"May the worst day 8 be better than the best day of your past!"

PALS: Part One

Dail Nelson Nelson
2014

PALS: Part One

By

David Nelson Nelson

Cowboy Poet Press
2013

Copyright © 2013 by David Nelson Nelson
www.davidnelsonauthor.com

All rights reserved. This book or any portion thereof may not be reproduced or used in any manner whatsoever without the express written permission of the author except for brief quotations in a book review.

Printed in the United States of America

First Printing 2013

ISBN-13: 978-1492822530
ISBN-10: 1492822531

Cowboy Poet Press

A special note of thanks to my support team:

    Gretchen Houser: Editor

    Carl Short: Wed Designer, Technical Support

    Maggie Tyler and Dr. Ellen Rudolph: Cover Design

    Bryan Mihalakis: Co-Contributor

    Richard "Rick" Nelson: Co-Contributor

* Any and all errors appearing in this book are mine alone and are not the responsibility of the Editor. David Nelson Nelson, Author

I dedicate my work to:

Jean Nelson, my wife
For her undying love and support of me and for being my best friend in life.

Richard "Rick" Nelson & Maggie Tyler
My brother and sister for their unfailing source of support and love. Many of my stories could not have been written without them.

The PALS

Bryan Mihalakis aka "Mean Boy"
For his wit, sarcasm, support and satire for the last fifty years

Becky Rafoth Smith
For her guidance, love, support and patience for over fifty years

Dave Markward
For his friendship, his laughter at my jokes, for demonstrating how to take the right path, and his lifelong support.

Rich Clemens
For his pranks, his jokes and unbridled sense of humor. My Pal also for over fifty years.

Tom Schweikert
For his lifelong friendship, constant support, for the safety of his home and family, and for allowing me to be his "brother" for over fifty years.

Table of Contents

Introduction 4
   "Huey's" 9
   "The Flats" 15
SECTION I 21
   Audubon Elementary School 21
      "Randy Has a Rock" 22
      "Dick and Jane" 26
      "The Greatest Invention" 30
      "Tom" 35
      "What's Beyond the Nylons?" 40
      "Fire Prevention" 43
      "The Great Contest" 47
      "Silent Night, Holy Night" 50
      "Hocking" 52
      "School Patrol" 55
      "Ping Pong Anyone?" 57
      "Run! He's Going for the Knives!" 61
      "How's the Watermelon and What's That Noise?" 63
      "Bums and BBs" 69
      "Violins and Trains" 72
      "Life Lessons Learned" 77
Section II 80
   Jefferson Junior High School 80
      "The Melting Pot" 81
      "Homeroom Number 107" 86
      "The Christmas Tree" 91

"Physical Education" 94
"The Great Paint Fight" 97
"Linwood Cemetery, Pop, Marilyn" 105
"Twice a Day Confessions" 113
"Baking Bulbs" 116
"Boners, Farts and Peeing Contests" 120
"Bobo: The Lucky Strike Chimp" 128
"Changing the Way America Does Business" 133
"The Dubuque Packers" 138
"Popeye" 141
"You Should Stick to Track" 144
"Jesse Owens" 148
"He Winds Up. Here's the Pitch" 152
"Gems and Thefts" 158
"Auto Theft and Bombs" 164
"The Bridge Jump" 168
"The Spring Thaw" 172
"Put Out or Get Out" 177
"On My Honor" 181
"Phocomelia" 184
"Getting Even" 189
"Shoes & Pews" 191
"Preparing for Departure" 194
"Life Lessons Learned" 196

Section III 199
Dubuque Senior High School 199
"Smoking" 200
"Wareco" 206

"Looking Good" 209
"Fill It Up" 211
"Bowling" 215
"Henry Stole My Rabbits" 218
"The Edsel" 228
"The Empty Pear Tree" 241
"The War" 245
"Beyond Pomp and Circumstance" 247
Epilogue 249
Appendix 252

David Nelson Nelson

Introduction

Dubuque, Iowa is the oldest city in Iowa. I lived in one of the oldest parts of town called the North End. Life in the North End during the late 1950s and early 1960s was different than the rest of Dubuque. The North End was an impoverished pocket of alcoholic parents, manual laborers and large families. There was one family on Windsor Avenue around the corner from my house that had seventeen kids. Our family was spread out in ages where the older ones didn't really know our younger siblings because we had moved out of the house when they were young. There were seven of us kids. I was the third oldest.

The area was a mix of Catholic and non-Catholic families. From any place in my house and, as a matter of fact, any place in the entire neighborhood we would hear the bells of Sacred Heart that would resonate but not crack each day at noon and before each Mass. Dubuque has always been a predominantly Catholic city. It was almost a taboo for the religions to mix in marriage. If a non-Catholic married a Catholic, the mothers in the neighborhood gossiped for days about where the children would go to church or even attend school.

My parents made me attend St. Peter Lutheran Church just two blocks from home. They never attended. The church was located across the tracks from Boyce's Wrecking and Towing Company. Occasionally, a train would pass by and vibrate the stained glass windows. Often the minister had to yell his message over the rumbling locomotive. This was the church where I was confirmed after it moved to Asbury Road in Dubuque.

My roots in the Lutheran Church on the side of my "natural" father went quite deep. My great grandfather, born in Diebach, Germany was Dr. Johann Michael Reu (1869-1943). My brother, Richard's middle name is from Dr. Reu. My middle name of "Nelson" was the maiden name of my Grandmother on Ma's side. She was from Norway. Craig Nessan, former academic dean and professor of contextual theology at Wartburg Seminary once said of my great grandfather, "One might with much evidence name Dr. Reu the most prolific and renowned professor and theologian in the history of Wartburg Seminary."

It has been reported that Reu's Catechism was used by confirmands in the Church from 1906 until the 1970s. His influence was worldwide. Dr. Reu taught at the seminary from 1899 until his death in 1943. He was my grandmother's (gross mama's) father. My gross mama married my gross papa who was also influential in the Lutheran Church. Dr. Samuel Salzmann was a professor of homiletics for numerous decades. Their son, Richard (Dick) was my natural father. He was once a missionary in New Guinea. I saw Dick twice in my life. He and my mother divorced when I was weeks old. Dick Salzmann left the Dubuque area and moved to New York State where he was the Editor-in-Chief of the Research Institute of America located in Washington, D.C. After the divorce Ma married my Dad who adopted us. His last name was Nelson and consequently, I have the same middle and last name of "Nelson."

Many elders in the church knew my two older siblings and me quite well. They seemed to keep an eye on us for some reason. This included Coach Udelhoff from Jefferson Junior High School, who was a member there. It was not until I was an adult that I learned my family history. Family secrets were to be kept in the closet in the 1950s. A divorced woman was a tainted woman. I was not allowed to play with one friend, Leroy because his mother was divorced and never re-married. He and I sure had lots of fun together.

For a few years, I was an acolyte and a member of the children's choir. We were required to wear a white, fluffy top and a black dress that covered our church clothes. Strangely, I didn't mind the dress. As a matter of fact many times in my life at Halloween I have gone in drag. I guess I have the church to blame for that.

I was always terrified of not being able to light the candles that were on the altar. We followed the strict guideline of holding the gold-plated rod with the lighted wick on the end, with one hand,

and cupping the sacred flame with the other. The fear of one or more candles going out created quite the stress for a small nervous boy like me. God, forbid, if the flame went out we would not receive any green Jello with little marshmallows at the after-church potluck luncheon. Green Jello with tiny white marshmallows and German potato salad are staples at all Lutheran potlucks.

The honor of being an acolyte was given only to boys and we served a month at a time. Often, my pal Tom followed me in the rotation. On my last service of the month I would try to leave my mark. I pinched, twisted, and bent the wick so it would be difficult, if not impossible to light the following Sunday. I kept this a secret until just now. All those times of watching him struggle made me snicker, as it does now. Sorry, Tom.

I think I was both tone deaf and dyslexic back then. I know for certain I am now. I could clean out a room with a solo piece of *"A Mighty Fortress Is Our God"* in less than two minutes. The minister said people were too slow leaving the church after service, so he had me sing many solos. Between the two of us, we got the job done. The junkyard dog whined and crawled under a 1949 Plymouth, old ladies fainted, old men turned down their hearing aids, and children laughed. I was given extra green Jello from my friends whenever I sang.

The families in the North End were mostly hardworking lower middle class Germans. There were also low class families who smelled from fuel oil, had no lunch at school and some had dirt floors in their basements. There were many who were uneducated and several who were racists. I heard the word "Negro" used often. Only it was not "Negro." Our fathers used the word once in a while at the supper table, older boys called younger ones by that name and sometimes when us little kids were mad we imitated what we had learned. I heard for years that, at one time Dubuque was the largest segregated city north of the Mason-Dixon line. I don't know if that's true, but with a population of 50,000 people there was only one family of African-Americans.

PALS: Part One

The North End was the home of America's first Heisman Trophy Winner, Jay Berwanger. He attended the same junior and senior high schools as I did. He played football for the University of Chicago and was awarded the Heisman Trophy in 1935.

Every region in America has its own colloquialism with phrases or words. I'm not certain if the rest of Dubuquers spoke like some of the families in the North End. I supposed it was remnants of the German ancestry when wash was called *"warsh."* I would hear *"Jeet Ye?"* That meant, "Did you eat yet?" Then was *"gunna"* for going to. When speaking to a single person or a group, it was common to hear *"youse guys."*

There was a time when Dubuque was second in per capita consumption of beer behind Munich, Germany. All Dubuquers love their beer. When I was young I saw the fathers drinking beers like Dubuque's own, Star Beer. They may have consumed Potosi Beer from nearby Wisconsin. There was also Hamm's, Schlitz and Pabst. What would go better with beer than a good game of euchre?

There is still some debate as to its origin. Some say specifically, Germany. Other reports say Canada and South Africa. This fast paced card game of taking tricks and making points, is known by almost every Dubuquer. There are euchre tournaments every Saturday evening in bars throughout the North End. Some German bars might play music from Leo Greco. Some folks loved the polka music. Greco entertained generations playing his accordion and hosting his "Variety Time" program on radio station WMT-AM.

From my house at 617 Lincoln Avenue we could hear the squealing of hogs and the bellowing of cows about to be slaughtered at one of the largest employers in Dubuque and the largest independent meat packing plant in America. It was called the Dubuque Packing House. We simply referred to it as just the "Pack." If parents didn't work at the Pack, they worked at the other large employer – John Deere. I had one pal whose mother worked outside the home. Most of the mothers did not. My mother, however, worked for a short time until she had another "nervous spell."

All the houses had either green or red roofs with steep pitches. Many houses were an arm's length away from the neighbor's house. There were almost no front yards and the back yards were long and narrow. My house was built in 1890. The lot size measured twenty-six feet wide and one hundred-thirty-eight feet long. Three doors away was a house that once was a horse stable and blacksmith shop. For the most part homes were heated with coal or oil. Our house was drafty in the winter and stifling in the summer. We had no air conditioning.

Each day we heard the rumbling of trains past our houses and smelled the oil cars from the railroad maintenance yards two blocks away. Bums or Hobos were a daily sight that we ignored as kids. We also ignored drunks who pissed or shit their pants and were unconscious on the sidewalks where we roller-skated or played tag.

We did not, however, ignore older kids who were on the hunt to beat up younger children. I learned at an early age that I had the gift of being able to run fast. I used that gift many times to outrun an older thug. On one occasion the meanest kid in our neighborhood said I was not allowed to play baseball because I was too small. He pissed me off, so I took a brick and chased after him. Even though he had a head start, I caught up and threw the brick almost hitting his head. I sprinted passed him and ran up the alleyway behind our house. I knew he would come looking for me so I hid inside an empty metal trashcan. He never bothered me again.

If we had a bicycle, it had no fenders, patched tires and often we rode double with a buddy on the front handlebars. Sometimes we stole bikes from other kids. The accepted way to summon a friend to come and play was to stand outside his house and yell his name repeatedly. We never knocked on the door or rang a doorbell. We just stood there bellowing until he came out to play or his mother shouted out the window that he was gone. Often, the mothers would yell for us to shut up and get the hell out of there.

"Huey's"
by Richard "Rick" Reu Nelson

In 1957, our territory on the North End of Dubuque was not a great expanse. Our roaming was bounded on the north by Windsor Avenue, by Rhomberg on the east, Kniest on the south, and East 22nd to the west. Movement beyond those limits was by express permission only. However, if an eight-year-old was daring enough, he could always sneak past the lines of motherly defense, brave the dangers of traffic, and find himself off the map, exploring the vastness beyond the Audubon School playground. If you got caught, the penalty was severe: we'd all felt the sting of a newly snapped and skinned lilac switch smartly applied to the tiny buttock. But we had to face the danger; we had no choice. We were boys and the threat of whizzing cars and the whistling of the switch is just too small a thing to dampen the wanderlust of young boys. And ours was a wanderlust sharpened and amplified by the knowledge that out there, beyond the pale, was an El Dorado worth risking it all to find: Kress's Confectionary.

Had we been able to search the world over, no cache of gold and silver could equal the treasures to be found in Kress's: Duncan yo-yos; black licorice, two for a penny; High Flier kites; hard penny candy; packs of Topp's baseball cards, five cents each; seven-ounce bottles of Coca-Cola and Bubble-Up; ice cream sodas for one fat quarter. So many delights that no amount of money or appetite could ever consume. Kress's was located on the corner of East 22nd and Johnson Street. The children in the neighborhood called it Huey's, after the owner and operator, the man behind the counter whose life's work it was, it seemed, to stock every luxury a child could imagine.

It wasn't until I was seven or so that I even realized Huey's store had another name, or that it offered bread, bologna, and milk along with gumdrops, malted milk balls and solid rubber baseballs that ached for the pulverizing swat of a junior Louisville slugger (and which would eventually be lost to the roof of Audubon, there to disintegrate in the sun and rain).

Huey's store was old. At least the building was old. On the outer wall a barely visible sign painted in red, white and blue advertised Wonder Bread ("Helps Build Strong Bodies in 8 Ways"). Years of bouncing rubber balls off the wall and catching them in the middle of Johnson Street had chipped most of the paint from the pitted bricks. However, the age of the building belied the newness of its riches.

On either side of the entryway, two dimly lighted glass cases exhibited the newest toys and comic books. Behind the glass cases, built-in wooden shelves from floor to ceiling housed a greater assortment of bright red wax lips, candy cigarettes, bubble gum cigars, jacks, pencils, notebooks, and binders. Directly opposite stood a marble-topped counter protecting the cold cavernous cylinders of genuine chocolate, strawberry, vanilla, and black raspberry flavored ice cream. While an ambulatory towhead was free to wander throughout the store (an excursion that could take anywhere from a minute to an hour), no one crossed the marble barrier except Huey. You'd pay your nickel, he'd go behind the counter, and roll a perfect ball of ice cream into the scoop and place it just so on top of a wafer cone. Two scoops went for seven cents.

Between the display cases and the frozen delights was an aisle; at least, that is what it should have been. Not in Huey's, however. That space of no more than ten by fifteen feet was occupied by a jungle of wire racks and baskets where tiny bodies could get lost examining the latest in genuine, imitation leather, miniature big league gloves—a buck twenty-five and balsa gliders (one fat quarter, and one skinny dime). Such was Huey's store, a small consumer paradise in the middle of a denying, abusive, oppressive parental inferno.

If a nickel could not be earned, the drainage ditch at the far south end of Audubon School almost always yielded a two-cent deposit pop bottle discarded by some extravagant teenager. Huey kept stacks of pop bottles in crates out back of his store, surrounded by a wooden seven-foot fence. It had a gate that was locked only at night from intruders in the alley. He kept it latched during the day.

PALS: Part One

We never believed adults fully appreciated the essence of Huey's. How could they? They would rush in for a pack of Lucky Strike cigarettes. Part of the tobacco industry's advertising slogan was L.S.M.F.T. That was an acronym for Lucky Strike Means Fine Tobacco. The adults would also buy a quart of Hilldale milk without ever stopping to scan the latest Tarzan comic book through a pair of colored cellophane 3-D glasses that cost fifteen cents.

David Nelson Nelson

As kids we drank from garden hoses. Often the first few seconds of water was hot from the sun on the hose and usually had bugs that were washed out with the initial water pressure. We were held back in school if we could not meet the standards, and we rode bicycles without helmets. There was lead in our painted cribs and lead in our gas. We believed in our President and Congress. We never questioned authority. If we were spanked at school we were spanked or beaten by our fathers when we went home. We could buy cigarettes for our parents at the neighborhood grocery store as long as there was a written note. These same stores would deliver to our houses. The doctor would come to our homes, as did the milkman and the iceman, who delivered ice in blocks for the icebox.

Some people had party lines for their telephones where two or more families used the same line. My phone number was 31037. We had only push lawn mowers with rotary blades. We tried out for baseball and not everyone was chosen to play. Trophies were not given to winners. Boys were taught not to cry. There was one bathtub for families as large as seventeen kids. Bras were worn on the outside of a sweater during television commercials. Armpits could not be exposed for deodorant commercials.

Children were to be seen and not heard. We were never allowed to miss school. It was "cool" to smoke. We would eat all the fish we caught. Our parents worked the same job their entire adult lives. The flat-head V8 engine was simple and owners did their own repairs. Doors to our houses were left unlocked twenty-four hours a day. It was safe to hitchhike.

My parents were alcoholics and Ma was mentally ill. She suffered severe bouts of depression that were magnified with the beer. I lived in a constant state of tension wondering if I'd be beaten again each night. The tension was accompanied with depression and sadness. I suspect the roots of my life-long clinical depression started at that time. My brothers and I were beaten with belts, kicked with steel-toed work boots, forced to stand at attention in the corners of a room. We had to take two steps back, lean into the corner with only our heads for support and our arms hung at our sides. This position was assumed for one hour on many occasions.

I was constantly told I was a no good dirty son-of-a-bitch and would never amount to a damn. One time my dad locked me away behind a cellar door. The steps inside connected the cellar to the outside above. The doors at the top and bottom were locked. My dad saw to that. I spent some eighteen hours alone in total blackness with only insects and severe heat to accompany me. I was eight years old.

I'm convinced there was an element in my personality that balanced my need to be amusing and entertaining. It was my sorrow that gave depth to my humor. I was known as the class clown while all the time hurting inside due to the physical abuse and absence of maternal nurturing.

PALS: Part One is a story of friendship involving five boys and one girl. It is a story about how this group became friends at an early age and remained friends over fifty years later. It is a story of conflict, trauma, and escape. It is a story of love, respect, laughter, pranks, and life. It is my story. To an outsider, my life might seem abominable. To me it was normal.

You will be there the morning we heard that Marilyn Monroe died. There will be egg and watermelon throwing, fart lighting, booby squeezing, and pastry stealing along the way as you join me in my past ventures. You will be there for a peeing contest. There will be boners, train hopping, and bridge jumping. You will hear the ice breaking on the Mississippi River during a spring thaw. You will learn how I changed the ways some American businesses operate. This includes the telephone company, Coca-Cola, the auto industry and a few more.

We could walk anywhere in Dubuque and feel safe- except for the Flats, which was an adjoining neighborhood to mine. We walked everywhere- except for the Flats.

David Nelson Nelson

By the way, Jay Berwanger was the only Heisman recipient who was tackled by a future President of the United States. It was Gerald Ford during a game between Michigan and the University of Chicago. President Ford reported years later he received a bloody nose and still had the scar to prove it.

PALS: Part One

"The Flats"
by Bryan Mihalakis

What constituted the Flats area was different according to where some people actually lived. Some folks who lived on Elm, Washington, Jackson, and White Streets considered their neighborhood a part of the Flats. But to my neighbors and me, the boundary of where the Flats began was simple: the railroad tracks. Everything east of the tracks was the Flats and everything west was a completely different world.

The Flats to us was bounded by the Milwaukee Road railroad maintenance shops and a switchyard that ran north and south until 18th Street, where it veered to the northeast out to the Municipal swimming pool, and then north again towards Minnesota. Adjacent to the railroad shops and yard was the stockyards for the Dubuque Packing Company where they received all of the animals prior to slaughtering them. Next to the stockyards was the main plant that covered a significant portion of the area and rose high above the neighborhood of small homes. To the east was the city dump that ran along 16th Street when I was young. What wasn't part of the city dump, were wetlands from the adjacent Mississippi River.

There was City Island, which included the Yacht Basin, the dump, the first airport in Dubuque, The Sports Bowl stock car racing, and the water ski club. On the eastern banks of the Mississippi were cottages built during the early part of the 20th century. The most famous was Camp Seventeen, as each of the cottages had a number. Nobody knew why Camp Seventeen was famous, but it seemed like everyone in Dubuque knew about it. There were also a number of floating boat-houses and boat docks spread along in the Peosta Channel.

South of 16th Street were more wetlands and the area where the storm sewers of Dubuque emptied. The southern boundaries of the Flats were the A.Y. McDonald brass foundry, the Caradco warehouse, and the Interstate Power Company plant. While the western boundary of the Flats was the railroad tracks, there was an industrial buffer on the west side of the tracks that separated the area before once again, homes appeared. From 18th Street south were the Metz Manufacturing Company, Max Blum's junkyard, the Decker Coal yards, the Municipal Garage, Jacobson's Junkyard and then the outcropping buildings of Caradco.

The Flats was the only neighborhood in Dubuque completely surrounded by heavy industry, which subjected the inhabitants to the terrible smells, polluted air, the never-ending noises, and the heavy traffic created by these companies. This area is where I grew up and it meant many things to us: our playground, where we worked, and where we lived.

As children most of us had little oversight and no supervision. We went out of the house in the morning only stopping back to eat lunch or supper and then we'd be off again until it was time to be back home at night. It was a little like a "Lord of the Flies" existence except you returned home at night We were street kids and we knew every inch of the area and just about every inch of every industrial facility. Packs of us kids would venture into all of these buildings looking to see what was going on and what we could possibly steal and sell at the local scrapyards. The scrapyards would not buy from us kids directly so we had to sell to a neighbor who lived next door to me and who had a junkyard in his backyard.

One of the few times we ventured out of our neighborhoods was to go to the Boys Club. We walked in a pack, stayed all day at the Club and then walked home at night when it closed. We would sometimes use the excuse that we were going to the Boys Club for the day and to be out of the range of our parents. In reality, at ten years old we would sometimes go shoe shining in the bars that lined lower Central Avenue and lower Main Street. We walked among the adults, many who were drunk. We offered to shine their shoes. We charged them twenty-five cents. Oftentimes, they would pay us fifty-cents – especially if they were trying to impress the woman sitting on the bar stool next to them. The key to shoe shining was to sneak into the bar and get someone to agree to a shine before the bartender saw us and kicked us out of the bar. If you already had a customer the bartenders would leave you alone. Shining was a lucrative business. On a good night we could make as much as a factory worker. Not bad for a ten year old.

Other than the weekends, there were always the sounds of the railroad in our daily lives. The freight trains passed by periodically during the day while switch engines spent the days and nights until midnight putting trains together. Waiting for trains to pass by was an everyday thing. We adapted by becoming proficient at crossing in front of the moving trains or riding them to where we wanted to go. Sometimes we would "scooch" under the stopped trains while people in the cars would look at us like we were crazy. But we knew how trains worked and nobody ever got hurt. One time, however, I jumped off one in the dark and immediately ran into a lantern holder. Bam!

When I was very young I remembered passenger trains coming through the neighborhood filled with military troops returning from Korea. The trains would sit there for an hour or so until they moved out. Soldiers would pay us twenty-five cents to run to the grocery store a block away and buy them things like ice cream. Glad to be home, they were big tippers and many of them would throw loose change on the ground for us to collect. At other times I saw African-American families passing by in a freight car, the door wide open while they were all perched in the doorway like they were posing for a photograph. Hanging out around the tracks and climbing in and out of the freight cars, we ran into hobos. We would run home, make a sandwich, steal cigarettes from our parents, and return to listen to their endless stories.

The smell of the packinghouse was a sickening odor we adjusted to, as it was ever-present. Those coming into our neighborhood would immediately notice the smell of dead animals, excrement ground into the streets where we played, the vapors of hides and guts, while blood permeated every crack and crevice in the four square block area. A.Y. McDonald factory had a steady stream of black smoke spewing out its chimneys, which was only a problem when the wind blew from the south. Everyone's laundry hanging outside often was covered in black, hard-to-remove, soot. Kids in the Flats seldom received any money from their parents. If we wanted money for pop, chips, ice cream, or the pinball machine we had to figure ways to get it. One thing we did was to scrap for brass from the A.Y. McDonald Company. Many days we made more money than a full-time worker at the Pack.

We also went junking where we would occasionally find a gondola. This was a boxcar without a top. It would be filled with scrap metal and if there were no Dicks around one of us would climb on top, throw out what he could and the rest of us would grab it and run like hell. Later we split all the profits after selling the stuff to older guys who in turn sold it back to the junkyards. We were the first people in America to re-cycle, so to speak.

Another way to make money was to collect pop bottles and turn them in for the cooperage. The best place to do this was where the young men worked on their stock cars at night. I had a special route and would some days make quite a bit of money picking up the pop bottles they threw away the night before. We walked the factories and foundries every day looking for any kind of metal. If we didn't have to crawl over or under a fence or if it wasn't fastened down in some fashion, it was fair game.

One time an older kid ruined the fresh paint job on a "scrammie" I'd just made. A "scrammie" is a push type version of a stock car. Like everything else in my life, I knew I had to handle this older kid by myself. I found a long lead pipe and hunted him down. When he turned toward me, I hit him as hard as I could smack-dab on the shins. He never again bothered me. Show 'em what you're made of, that was the lesson I'd learned. To survive this kind of environment, one learns to never back down. Better to get your ass kicked once, than to be picked on for an eternity. When a bully gets in your face you immediately get back in his or her face. I compare it to prison and the idea of respect. Being civilized about threatening situations can be fatal. By the time I was twelve I was a definite street-smart kid.

The Flats was strictly a blue collar neighborhood, a mixture of Catholics, a few non-Catholics (Protestants) and a significant portion that never saw the inside of a church except for funerals and weddings. Sex was a taboo subject in the homes and schools so we learned about the mysterious process sitting on a street corner at the feet of the "Big Kids." In every poor neighborhood there are the bulk of children who are basically good kids. Then, there is a smaller portion who are the source of most of the problems, brutality and anti-social behavior. There were usually the "Big Kids" who pontificated to the group of which we were a part, young with eager ears lapping up all the details. The "Big Kids" would go into descriptions of their sexual exploits, most of which would land someone in prison today. Many of their stories were pure machismo and bragging on their part. And some were not. Some were true stories of sexual brutality that no ten year old should be listening to or even be aware of that bad behavior.

My dad worked all the time and my mom spent the day trying to raise nine kids. Many of the parents had large families and low budgets. By the time many of them were able to relax at night, they did not want to be troubled with the problems of their children. Many of the parents walked to the Airport Inn and for a few hours had a few beers and talked with neighbors. They would come home feeling a buzz, go to bed and the next day do it all over again tomorrow. Children in the Flats did not receive much nurturing, empathy for our problems or attention. This lifestyle made you tough and taught you to solve your own problems or suffer them. The Streets devour the weak. That was the case of some of the children in the neighborhood. This lifestyle was the formula for creating a kid with "street smarts." And I became such a kid and then an adult that has served me well travelling around the world by myself in third world countries.

Growing up in poverty and in a dysfunctional environment lacking the nurturing and protection that all children need, has a tendency to create anxiety filled individuals that learn to live by doing whatever is necessary to survive. Many times this is exhibited through anti-social behavior. "Fight or Flight" comes to the forefront often. Children are always on the lookout for any opportunity, danger or threats on their horizon. This attitude provides them instinct and the ability to survive on their own. Sensitivity to others is an unaffordable luxury at times.

David Nelson Nelson

"Some children experience their childhood and then spend the rest of their lives trying to get over it."
-Unknown

PALS: Part One

SECTION I

Audubon Elementary School

David Nelson Nelson

"Randy Has a Rock"

I don't remember the name of my kindergarten teacher at Audubon Elementary School. But I do remember the coatroom, the huge clock on the wall, the desks with inkwells and the picture of Abraham Lincoln over the door. I also remember a lot of noise as I suppose was to be expected from five-year old kids. We recited the Pledge of Allegiance to the flag hanging next to the door.

Why we had inkwells is anybody's guess. We didn't know how to print and we didn't know what ink was used for in those days. The coatroom spanned the entire width of the classroom except the two open doorways at each end. We had our own hooks where we hung our parkas and neatly placed our snow boots. The hooks were black metal and the wood supporting them was made of oak. We were good at following directions, lining up single file, and marching into one doorway only to shed our outer garments and then march out the other side. In all other seasons besides winter and rainstorms, the area was never used.

I suspect all that marching was somehow left over from WWII. The North End of Dubuque, Iowa was full of two things: veterans and people of German descent. There were family names like Kuperschmidt, Udelhoven, Koernschield, Schmidt, Smaltz, Wagner, and many others. We learned to stand up straight, march in unison and never question authority.

And then the huge, wooden door squeaked open and there entered the meanest, scariest, and strongest woman I ever saw. Elsie Schroeder was our principal and seemed to even frighten the teacher who stopped reading to us and stood at attention. She welcomed us to Audubon and told us the rules as she had to other students for the past 40 years. We sat on the floor looking up at her and unable to stop staring at her wide nostrils and thick nose. I was seated in the front of the semi-circle and had to strain to look up at this giant woman. I noticed a hardened booger in her left nostril. I thought it was funny. Each time she started a new sentence, that booger moved back and forth like a baseball card hooked with a clothespin to the spokes on my bicycle. It made a rat-tat-tat noise. She had stump-like fingers and fat calves that were draped from above with a black dress that dropped mid-way to her ankles. She wore black shoes with wide heels that supported her 250-pound frame. The inlaid oak floor crunched and bent (but did not break) as she sauntered among us. She had huge, thick lips that went from below her nose to her chin. Those big lips must have helped her to enunciate each and every syllable. She spoke slowly and with great intention. She smelled like a combination of my musty-smelling cellar and burnt sauerkraut. She showed us the dreaded wind-whipper.

The wind-whipper was a four-inch wide paddle with six holes cut into its fourteen-inch length of solid oak. It was tapered at the end allowing a firm grip with which to paddle children. We had heard stories about that paddle from our older siblings or kids in the neighborhood. Its name was derived from the fact that when she swung it through the air, one could hear the wind blowing through the holes. Swish, swish.

"Now I know I will never have to use this on any of you children," she said slapping it into her left palm while gripping the handle with her white-knuckled right hand. She continued, "But if you ever sass off to your teacher while here at Audubon I will burn your tiny butts hard with huge blisters. Do you understand me?"

"Yes, Miss Schroeder," we all said in unison as if we were saying the Pledge of Allegiance. She picked at her nostril with her thumb and index finger, turned, and left the room. The hardened oak door closed with a bang as the hinges squeaked behind her. We continued hearing the wind-whipper slap against her hand in the hallway, like she was looking for prey. About that time George Schmidt let out a shriek.

"Look, teacher. Randy has a rock and it stinks!"

I looked over to see Randy Schickelmyer holding up not a rock but a turd. When old Lady Schroeder came in to talk with us, she literally scared the shit out of him. What had been a neat and orderly semi-circle of five-year old boys and girls turned into a stampede like on the Roy Rogers' Television Show.

Three girls gave out simultaneous, high-pitched shrills that could have caused a dog to go berserk. Two others ran into the coatroom to hide. I saw one boy gagging, another laughing and pointing at Randy, while a third cupped his mouth with his hands and yelled, "Turd! Everybody run!"

All the kids were screaming, running in circles, pointing, gagging or laughing. I don't think Randy was too intelligent for a five-year old. He thought it was funny. He loved the attention. He was actually running around the classroom with that turd in his hand. When he cornered someone, he held up his morsel, laughed, and pushed it toward his face. That created even more pandemonium.

Even though I was only five, I had respect for authority. I suspect it was from my past experience and fear of the consequences if I did not obey. My dad taught me that. My old man was so frightening that when he yelled at one of us kids, all the others fell to the floor simultaneously. He could stop an attacking, snarling, and growling dog in its tracks with just his index finger. His voice could rumble and vibrate anything hanging on the walls two stories above the cellar where, on a regular basis he fought with the fuse box. The heck with all those starving kids in China come suppertime. If we held food in our mouths and refused to swallow, he would growl like an ogre hiding in an empty, fifty-gallon barrel. His commands created a fear that caused us kids to develop suction from our rectums up into our throats that was more powerful than a new Electrolux vacuum cleaner. Immediately our food shot a beeline for our guts. We feared him and consequently knew to follow orders.

That fear I had of the old man was the same fear I felt about Principal Schroeder. When the class went nuts, I stayed put. I sat perched on the floor with my legs bent at the knees exactly where I was when she left the room moments prior. I wanted to be certain that she knew I was not involved. Ah ha. The only change in my posture was that now I covered my nose and buried my face between my knees. One thing I knew by age five was to pick your battles and be certain a whipping was worth the action.

Just as the teacher reached Randy with a huge wad of paper towels, in came Miss Schroeder. She glanced at me for a split-second and screamed, "All right you children, sit down! Now!"

I was impressed with the reaction. It was just like at home. Twenty-one kids fell to the floor immediately. Those kids were spread-out in the room like dead soldiers on a battlefield. There would have been twenty-three children except the two girls in the coatroom who stood and peeked out at the action and hid again. Randy was standing and was being cleaned up by the teacher. Watching the kids fall to the floor reminded me of Penny and Sky King buzzing villains with their airplane, as they did every Saturday morning on television during the "Sky King Show." Inevitably, the villain also gave up – just like my classmates.

When Principal Schroeder heard what happened, she did not paddle Randy. I suspect she was smart enough to realize the wind-whipper would be covered in poop. I figured she also knew when to pick her battles and if a whipping was worth the action.

Randy was taken to the office and stood there silently until his mother could walk across the street from their home and bring clean clothes. That single event made me become a thinker before each attempt to break rules in Life.

A Cowboy Poem
There once was a cowboy named Clyde.
He fell through a hole in the privy and died.
Clyde had a brother who fell into the other.
Now, they're both in-turd side by side.

David Nelson Nelson

"Dick and Jane"

Who the heck were Dick & Jane? That's the book we used in first grade and how we learned to read at Audubon. I remember where the first grade room was located but I don't remember the teacher's name. The book, however, went something like this.

"See Jane."

"See Dick."

"See Jane run!"

"See Dick chase Jane!"

"See Dick catch Jane."

"See Dick and Jane French Kiss."

I just made that last part up. But I think the boys from the North End would have learned this lesson quicker had they used my version.

I probably would have enjoyed reading more if we'd read the Lone Ranger and Tonto or Superman and Lois Lane. If six-year old kids knew that Superman really was Clark Kent, why didn't Lois Lane also know? I learned critical thinking in the first grade. I was critical of others who could not read. Today, I realize that was wrong thinking.

It was at this time in my life I was introduced to a talking beaver with bucked-teeth on a television commercial. The advertisement promoted Ipana Toothpaste. I still remember the jingle. "Brush-a, Brush-a, Brush-a, Brush with new Ipana." We watched Mighty Mouse on Saturday mornings. That show was sponsored by Colgate toothpaste and it started with Mighty Mouse riding a tube of toothpaste into space. There must have been a lot of tooth decay in America.

A couple years later there was a commercial for "Hamm's Beer – the beer that is refreshing." It also featured a beaver, that chewed a tree down and it fell into a lake. Then a bear rolled on top of the log while drum music played in the background. It went something like, "From the land of sky blue water, Hamm's Beer..." I figured those beavers must have been alcoholics with severe tooth decay, or something.

I never had any difficulty learning to read, write, or perform arithmetic. To learn spelling we used acronyms in the first grade. I learned the word "arithmetic" by taking the first letter of each of the following words: "A rat in the house might eat the ice cream." The acronym for geography was spelled, "George Edward's old grandfather rode a pony home yesterday." Luckily, learning was always easy for me. It was staying focused, that was, at times difficult.

I am proud to have been educated in the most literate State in America. Dubuque, Iowa has always been known for its higher education and great scores on SAT and GRE Tests. There are two Catholic Colleges and one University affiliated with the Presbyterian Church. Wartburg Seminary is where Lutherans receive post-graduate training to become ministers.

My elementary school was one of the first schools constructed in Dubuque. The original name was the 5th Ward School and was built in 1854. The name was changed to Eagle Point School around 1884. The original school was razed in 1884 and a new one built on the same grounds. That was the school I attended some seventy years later. In 1889 the name was changed to Audubon Elementary School. In 1875, German language was taught because of the high numbers of German families in the North End.

Audubon had a basement with a classroom for children with special needs. That was a progressive step by the Board of Education. There was a kindergarten class, a music room, and an art room. The main floor had grades first through third, a library, and Principal Schroeder's Office. The third floor housed grades four through six while the top floor was the gymnasium. All floors were inlaid oak. Each door seemed to be seven feet tall, and had black, round metal handles. Some doors had smoked glass windows in them.

The gymnasium also had oak flooring, a stage for our annual Christmas Pageant, and two sets of double wood doors at each end opened with a brass handle across each door. In the gymnasium I learned a folk dance called the Maypole. Little did I know that one history report states that the Maypole dance began in ancient Babylon during sex worship and fertility rites! Why didn't we know that in elementary school? Another history report states the origin of the dance is from many countries including Germany, Sweden, and England. We each held a colored ribbon and walked slowly to music around a pole creating a multi-colored pole when completed. I don't know about you, but I'm still back on the fertility rites.

Each year at Christmas we sang the same songs, with the same story read to the audience, and with the same costumes. One year my sister's doll was used for Jesus. It was a girl doll, but nobody cared at that time. She called her doll Raggedy-Ann. The doll was such a hit at the nativity play that we began calling my sister the same name as the doll. All of us in my family had pet names we called one another. Some siblings did not think they were funny, so to keep peace, I will only tell you mine. My siblings called me Dumbo because I had ears that stuck out whenever I had my head shaved into a butch haircut by my old man in the backyard. Dumbo was an elephant character created by Walt Disney.

Some of the songs we sang during the Christmas Pageant included one that I still remember. "Star of wonder, star of night, guide us by the shining light. Westward leading, still proceeding take us to the place of light." I think I liked the melody and that is why I still remember it.

My pal, Tom and I created our own Christmas Carol. It went like this: "We three Kings of Orient Are, puffing on a rubber cigar. It was loaded and exploded BOOM! We two Kings of Orient Are, puffing on a rubber cigar. It was loaded and exploded BOOM! I one

King of Orient Are, puffing on a rubber cigar. It was loaded and exploded BOOM! Silent Night…"

I can assure you that if we knew more about that fertility dance around the Maypole, we would not have wasted our talents with silly songs.

David Nelson Nelson

"The Greatest Invention"

We each had a project to create in the second grade. We were expected to stand in front of the class and talk about it. There was no way I could ask my alcoholic parents for help. I had to come up with my own idea. Flash cameras were quite the rage back then. It was fun to watch the big bulbs explode catching a piece of history. It was also fun to watch the people taking pictures burn their fingertips when removing the scalding hot and then useless bulbs. They would jockey the hot bulb back and forth between one hand and another. The seasoned photographers would quickly move the scalding bulb among their fingers and thumb on just one hand waiting for it to cool. I especially liked that part. The whole process reminded me of the St. Vitus Dance.

My idea was to make my own version of a new camera. The supplies included a shoebox, aluminum foil, paper grocery sacks, colored pencils, and a set of encyclopedias. I stole the foil from the lower third drawer of our kitchen cabinets to the left of the sink. I hid the foil inside my woolen parka that day as I walked the half block to Audubon. I cut through Mrs. Cierney's yard and sat down in the snow with my back propped up against her dilapidated garage by the alley.

I had to hide out in there so I wouldn't be discovered creating my camera. Older kids might beat me up and destroy my work. Other mothers might tell Ma and I would be in real trouble. I could possibly get a whipping from the Old Man. Each yard had clotheslines strung across the grass and the lines held the long sticks with a 'v' cut into one end. It was the 'v' end that supported the line laden with clothes during warm months. Had this project been given to us during those times I would have easily hid behind the clothes. That particular day all the poles were neatly tucked away in garages, garages so rickety that they were almost falling down. But like an engineer at Eastman Kodak, I was laser focused on my invention.

A few days earlier I had taken paper grocery sacks and cut them to fit perfectly into the shoebox. Then I stole some of Ma's carbon paper and carefully traced pictures of animals I found in our set of Encyclopedia Britannica. After that I used the colored pencil set I got for Christmas from some nice guy at the Elk's Lodge. He adopted my family because we were poor. Those folks at the Lodge sure were kind to us, and a lot more families like us. They were a real Godsend. That year, all of us kids in my family had nice gifts.

I created an "ABCs of Animals." Each letter had a corresponding picture attached to it with tape. There I was with twenty-six pieces of old grocery sacks cut perfectly to fit into the shoe box. I colored each one, never once going over the traced lines. I placed each animal picture in order from A-Z into the box. I was bursting with pride that day sitting in the snow and putting it all together. The wind and sub-zero temperature never daunted me a bit. I crinkled the aluminum foil to give it the appearance of a futuristic camera. I covered the shoebox - lid and all. I ran to school knowing I would be the best in the class. I hung my winter coat on the hook in the coatroom, put my mittens in the pockets and removed my black rubber boots. Sitting in the back of the room, I could hardly wait for my turn to share my invention with the class.

Right after the pledge we started the big day. God, I was bored when all the other kids got up and did what I thought were stupid things. I felt that way because of "critical thinking" I learned a year earlier.

One kid made an ant killer with a magnifying glass he won from a Cracker-Jack box. All of us boys knew that old trick. Betsy demonstrated how to set a table correctly. That also was stupid. We were taught that activity at home. She even brought in a set of little dishes. I heard Miss Miller say, "Dave, it is your turn. Come to the front."

I walked past Anna Schultz who stuck her tongue out at me while I blew a puff of air through my pursed lips in her direction. Her tongue trick didn't offend me. I was going to be the best inventor that day.

I explained my "ABCs of Animals" and began to pull them from my "camera box." However, there was just one problem. I had wrapped the entire box in aluminum foil. I should have wrapped the big part of the box and then the top separately. My fingers fumbled as I tried prying off the lid. I was so upset I just ripped the lid off. There it was, my perfect invention with chunks of aluminum foil hanging off the cover. Parts of my camera box were bare of any covering at all. I tore some of the foil off the lid and attempted to patch the bare spots on the box. A roomful of snickers began. I bit my cheek and looked around to see who thought this was funny. They would go on my enemy-list for sure the next time we had playground. After making the corrections I was ready.

I told them, "A is for ape," as I made a clicking sound with my tongue as if to take a picture.

The entire class including, Miss Miller laughed as I held up a zebra. "Damn, Son of a Bitch!" I thought as I instantly realized I placed all animals into the box in the wrong order. I was a failure. Those cuss words were learned from the older boys who hung around at the elm tree on our playground. I also heard those words nightly from my dad at supper. That was my first attempt at public speaking. I was a failure. The laughter of all the kids and the teacher threw off my concentration and I fumbled my way to the end. Nobody clapped that day for me.

I was especially upset with Miss "Turkey" Miller for laughing at me. She was our teacher, but then again she was another adult that reinforced my anti-authority feelings. The reason we called her "Turkey" was her skin texture. It was all wrinkled and hung off her face and the fleshy growth met in the center of her throat. It looked exactly like a waddle on a turkey. It wiggled and flapped when she moved right and left. That skin was so heavy it pulled her jaw into the open position and that was where it remained. I still remember her long narrow face with the mouth stuck open and lipstick sometimes on her teeth.

She was another spinster schoolteacher who stunk. Whenever she'd lean over me to check my printing I'd hold my breath. The perfume was more than a boy of seven should have to bear. When I did have to finally breathe, I developed a technique of raising my tongue to the roof of my mouth and sucked air in without it going through my nose first. I never noticed the fumes of dead animals from the Pack that permeated our neighborhood. But I sure enough noticed and didn't like the strong stench from the lilac perfume those elementary school teachers wore. I wondered if that's why they always carried a lace hanky stuck in their sleeves or hooked to their bra straps. It could have been a way to avoid another teacher's perfume odor.

At 3:30 that afternoon I drug myself up the alley towards home when I came upon Mrs. Johnson burning trash in a fifty gallon barrel at the back side of her yard. The snow was blowing sideways and the only comfort I felt was turning my head to the left inside of my parka. I had to look with my right eye through the parka so I didn't trip. I'm not certain if it was humiliation from my camera disaster, or the Iowa winter that made me feel awful. Inside that hooded garment and all alone, I found comfort.

I asked Mrs. Johnson if I could throw something into her burn barrel. She kindly obliged. With mitten-covered hands I ripped and tore all the photos I had in the box. Like a Harlem Globetrotter, I did slam-dunks with each shred of paper I found in my small grip. Some scraps of my artwork fell to the ground and were pulverized by my black rubber boots. Other pieces fell into the opening of my boots that were not fastened, because I had been in a hurry to leave school that day.

There was melted snow and mud that surrounded the hot, rusty barrel. I slipped and slid as I cussed like no seven year-old in the history of mankind. Mrs. Johnson just stood there with her toothless mouth wide open and knew better than to say a thing. I was probably a miniature of her husband. We heard him beating her on a regular basis in other seasons when the windows were opened. The shoebox and papers burned away into ashes. The aluminum foil lost its luster and would not go away. The radiant dream of my special camera was now tarnished like the singed foil. My memory of that dreadful event was like the aluminum foil.

David Nelson Nelson

I have another aluminum foil memory that happened the following spring at Mother's Day. I cut little pictures out of magazines, and using flour and water I made a paste. I then pasted the pictures on to a piece of paper titled "Why I Love My Mom." Each picture represented something different. I then crinkled the foil and pulled it back straight. I curled the edges and ends around my pictures to keep them in place. Using discarded wrapping from a previous holiday, I wrapped it and gave to Ma. She opened it and said, "Uh-Huh."

Later I found my gift wadded up into a ball and stuck down in the garbage. Despite all the years that have passed, I still think of those events periodically when I use aluminum foil.

"Tom"

"Whoosh" was the sound of the Linwood Bus as it stopped high above our heads while we clung to the limestone walls of the storm sewer. My new friend, Tom and I had earlier exhaled as much air as our tiny lungs would allow and wedged ourselves into the sewer beneath East 22nd Street in Dubuque, Iowa. The year was 1957. We were eight years old.

Tom was a skinny kid, with long black hair held down with Brylcream. He wore black-rimmed glasses and just like his dad, he regularly pushed his glasses further up on the bridge of his nose, using his left index finger - even when it was not necessary. He was a friendly kid who cackled when he laughed, an almost devilish sound. It was easy to make him laugh. One of the sources of laughter for the both of us was his dad.

One would never realize Bob was a former MP in the Army during WWII. Sure, his low, gruff voice would scare the crap out of a stranger. That kid, Randy from kindergarten would have dropped a full load if he ever met Bob. Tom's dad was the funniest adult I ever met. He was quick with a joke and was kind to everyone. I enjoyed pulling his trigger finger that made him fart. Often he would say, "Up your poop scoop too with a golden shovel."

Tom and his family recently moved into the neighborhood from a small farming community named Sherrill. His mother was the kindest person I ever met. She would stop what she was doing, sit down and look in our eyes and listen to our stories. She would ask questions, and then she would laugh. It was one of the kindest things anyone had ever done for me. She cared about me and showed it. I felt safe in their home from the very first day.

Tom had two older sisters who also were quick to laugh. Especially when Bob answered the phone, "Stinky's Fish Market, Stinky speaking." Or "City Morgue. You stab 'em, we slab 'em."

Both of them laughed at my jokes and like Tom's mother, they would sit and listen to what I had to say. I liked them immediately. Little kids can tell when they are liked and when they are not.

Tom and his family lived in a duplex at 2126 Kniest Street. Across the street was one set of railroad tracks. When a train passed, all the dishes in the cupboard would rattle and we had to walk across the room and turn up the volume knob on the television. Tom was the only kid in the neighborhood who received an allowance. That was because his parents both worked. It was unusual for the mother to work back then. His mom worked night shift at the Dubuque Packing House and his dad worked the day shift at John Deere. It was Tom's allowance that led us into the sewer.

We were armed and ready for war toward any unsuspecting adult driving down East 22nd Street or walking on its sidewalks above our perch. Our weapons were bean shooters and our ammunition was a bag of uncooked, white beans. Tom used his thirty-five cents allowance to buy our weapons and ammo at Kress's Confectionary Store.

One block away from Huey's, the 150 year-old drain sewer caught the flow of rain and run-off from the entire North End. Fifteen feet from our perches was a flow of water that became an underground creek that emptied into the Mississippi River. Above us were cars and neighbors heading up towards Sacred Heart Catholic Church. Some went the other direction towards Kaufmann and Central Avenues. We were safe. Not a soul knew we hid below looking for action. "Whoosh" was the sound again as the bus moved away from the curb on its way toward Linwood Cemetery and Xavier Hospital.

"Fire now!" Tom cackled as we both shot a line drive into the ankle of the lady who just departed the bus and into our war zone.

There was no DMZ. Everybody was fair game. It didn't matter the age, gender or their station in life. We hit her in the ankle with a white bean from our bean shooters while clinging to our cavern

PALS: Part One

wall. She stopped to rub the right ankle with the top of her left shoe as if that would lessen the pain. She continued walking and we continued laughing.

That morning we played baseball at Audubon. The game was temporarily interrupted when the "ice-man" stopped on Johnson Street near first base. His 1940s truck had a bed that carried blocks of ice sitting on sawdust, and covered with a black, heavy tarp. We watched him use a huge set of tongs to snag the ice block which he carried it across the street and into a home. The family who lived there obviously had an icebox rather than a refrigerator. We knew we had less than one minute to jump onto the truck bed, use the ice pick, and break off chunks of ice. We never got caught.

Like always when ice was involved, Tom and I quit playing baseball and enjoyed sucking on our ice, while sitting on a rock wall across from Huey's. It was refreshing to feel the cold water melt against our tongues on one end of the ice while the other end dripped on to our shirts. What a great way to beat the heat, I thought. It was because of the ice that we came up with the idea of crawling into the stinky, but cool sewer. We could be cool and have fun.

"Hey, do you feel that?" I asked. "It's a train."

"Oh my gosh. Who'd ever think it would shake the ground down here in the sewer. Let's get off this wall and get out of the way in case the whole thing comes down," Tom demanded. He jumped down, pushed his glasses up on his nose and went to the corner for safety.

A second later we were perched at the top of the limestone pathway that led to the flowing creek of wastewater. Crumbs and chunks of limestone shook, wiggled, and dropped onto us from the walls above, where we had been perched to hit that lady in the ankle. Our tiny chests rumbled to the squeal of the Milwaukee Road train as its wheels moved toward the Dubuque Packing House a half mile away. The dinging of the railroad bell echoed in our bunker beneath the street. The red flashes of the lights lit up the shadows where we hunkered down while the fumes from the waiting cars above began to enter our lungs. We coughed and gagged. We had no choice but to re-climb the wall again and peek our little heads out of the drain sewer's opening. We were seeking fresh air.

"Holy Cow," Tom exclaimed. "Look at all those cars and that one pick-up truck from Mulgrew's Ice Company. They are just sitting there waiting to get smacked. Let's get our weapons and fire away. Whoever gets the first ten hits wins."

In an instant we were firing as our tongues pulled away from the straw-like opening and high velocity air pushed out against the bean waiting inside. We shot beans across the street at drivers waiting for the passing train. I tried to hit the driver of the coal truck but couldn't reach him. Then I took aim at the guy in the Molo Oil Company truck. Missed again.

One guy took a drag off his Camel Cigarette as I hit him right in the lip and caused ashes and the lit end to fall inside the car and onto his pants. A better shot was never made. I could never do that again in a million years. He looked toward us but did not see his enemy. I saw him look in the rear view mirror. He looked at the hedges next to the house above us. He flicked his damaged cigarette out on to the street and rubbed his lip waiting for the railroad crossing to clear.

I heard the ping of Tom's bean hit the door of Mulgrew's Ice Truck. The driver didn't flinch. So we both fired at him trying to hit him in the head. We tried arch shots, direct shots and even ricochet shots. The best we could do was hit his door. We couldn't hit him directly. Without a head shot, boredom set in and we quit. We dropped to the cool cement below and heard the crossing-arm lift and the caution bells stop. Eventually all traffic was back to its regular speed.

It would be two years when we were in the fifth grade that we returned to the same spot. It was never as much fun as the first time.

PALS: Part One

Tom and I made up our own words to songs and commercials. For the Lucky Strike slogan of L.S.M.F.T. ("Lucky Strike Means Fine Tobacco") our version was "Loose Straps Mean Floppy Teats"

David Nelson Nelson

"What's Beyond the Nylons?"

Homes located in the North End, like the schools, were heated either with fuel oil or coal. Some homes had no source of heat to combat the 20 degrees below zero, which was normal during the winter. Audubon used steam from the coal furnace in the basement. There were no storm windows on the school to block the north winds and whoever sat next to them shivered like some of our fathers who went a day without alcohol. The windows were six-feet tall and over three-feet wide. They were double decker style where one set was placed on top of the other. The bottom set was the only one that could open. The best part of these windows was "the stick."

It was a three-foot long, rounded, piece of oak. On one end, the janitor, Merle, made a rubber handle for it, and the other end he'd fashioned had a 'J-shaped' hook. When the teacher left a room, we would scramble for the stick and pretend we were one of the Three Musketeers. I liked to think I was the pirate, Black Beard. While we were busy being adventurous, one kid squatted down and opened the massive wooden door two inches so he could stand guard and watch for the teacher to return. We would wave the pretend saber overhead and threaten other kids who tried to pry it from our hands.

I preferred using it to pretend stabbing my captors, who were naturally girls. They screamed like the irritating screeching sound of a train coming to a halt. There were always a couple of tattlers who exposed us. Boy, my old man could have had a hay-day with the tattling. If we had pulled antics like that at home, we would have beaten mercilessly.

Teachers had to step on a desk seat to reach the black metal clasps that locked the windows shut. They then used the stick to lock or unlock the window. Depending on the height of that teacher, she might have to get on her tiptoes and stretch or could stand flatfooted to reach the lock with the stick. I was thankful that my third grade teacher, Miss Phifner was short. I was also thankful for

PALS: Part One

having a seat in the window row. She was young, she was pretty, and had great legs.

There she was balancing on her toes, knees straightened like a hurdler, arms out stretched overhead, and her tiny frame was arched backwards to reach the lock with the stick. "Oh my God," I thought as I about fell out of my chair leaning left to look up her dress. With my wolf eyes I slowly traced her nylons from her ankles up into her tightened calves and above those knees up into her slender thighs. At the end of the nylons was a three-inch swath of darker material held up with a white plastic clamp.

One time, to catch a better view, I leaned so far left that my desk and I crashed to the floor. The laughter and ensuing pandemonium in the classroom was greater than any swashbuckling sword fight. The noise vibrated the windows and it wasn't long before the dreaded Miss Schroeder entered. She was slapping her opened left palm with (you guessed it) the wind-whipper. But I didn't care as I was in paradise. Locked inside my desk lying sideways on the inlaid, oak floor I saw it. It was Miss Phifner's garter belt.

I felt the hands of two of the biggest kids in class grab my desk from each side. They lifted me, and my desk in one piece, and placed it back in the correct position. Both kids were holding in giggles. I continued to crane my neck as slowly the awesome view disappeared from sight. The class was now silent, but Elsie Schroeder was not.

"Dave, this hurts me more than you. You know the position," she said as she gave her palm one final smack before laying it to my backside.

I bent forward and grabbed my ankles. A small swatch of cloth protected my supple cheeks from the oak paddle. Ten hard licks - that was the rule. The class was sullen. I was thinking how that burn was nothing compared to what I got at home from either end of my dad's belt, as welts began to raise on each little rump cheek.

David Nelson Nelson

Elsie Schroeder spoke those dreaded words. "Now did we learn a lesson today, Dave?"

"Yes I did." I responded while rubbing my cheeks and returned to my desk. I need to brace myself better against the desk. That was my lesson, I thought.

What the principal didn't know was I wished the class had not laughed because I might have spotted Miss Phifner's panties. I sure slept great that night.

So this fella walks into a bakery shop and asks the young lady for some raisin bread. She climbs the ladder and reaches for some bread and her dress opens up as she reaches high above for the item. He looks up her dress. On the way out he tells the next fella to order raisin bread. He does and also enjoys the view. On his way out he tells an old fella, wobbling with a cane to do the same. The young lady is still on the ladder and asks if his is raisin too. He responds, "No, but it's a quivering a bit!" (Sorry folks, I can't help myself).

PALS: Part One

"Fire Prevention"

In the fall of third grade there was a contest for all children sponsored by the City of Dubuque Fire Department and the school system. Each of us was offered an opportunity to write a slogan about fire prevention. The winners would be given a personal tour of the firehouse on 11th Avenue across from the Dubuque Boys' Club and each would be made honorary officers. I had a difficult time completing my slogan and asked my older brother, Richard to help me. He was such a great asset. In nothing flat he wrote the second half of my two-line slogan. I submitted it and forgot all about the contest. I was too focused on Miss Phifner and trying diligently to practice thirty degrees leaning port side in my desk without falling over again.

"Children, I have an announcement to make," Principal Schroeder said as she interrupted our class. "Dave has won third place in the Dubuque Fire Slogan Contest. Let's all give him a hand."

The applause ended just as I finished my practice session of leaning with my desk. I caught my desk with my right foot and raised my hand. "Miss Schroeder, I didn't write all of that. My brother, Richard in the fifth grade wrote part of it," I said proudly hoping he would get some credit.

She covered her mouth with her right palm and immediately left the room. I just knew she was excited for both of us. I figured Richard would be so proud when I told him later in the day. But sadly that was not to be.

"Ouch, that's hot!" I yelled as Richard sprayed me later with hot water from a garden hose that was heated during that hot September day.

We stopped for a drink of water from Mrs. Johnson's hose hooked to a spigot on the side of her house. After a moment he said, "Hey, look at this. It's a worm coming out of the hose. Must have been hiding all day. I wonder if Darin and I could look into all the hoses and find worms for our night crawler collection."

Richard and Darin O'Meara caught worms that were known by everyone as night crawlers. They kept them in buckets and covered the worms with coffee grounds and dirt. Just through word of mouth, they sold lots of them for bait and made pretty good money for fifth graders.

The water finally cooled enough to drink. He finished getting his drink and once again sprayed me with the water using his thumb on the hose's end. This time it was cold. "Hey what the heck are you doing? That's cold," I yelled.

"What the hell did you tell "Sacajawea" today in class?" He asked as we walked the half block home. Sacajawea was our secret pet name for the principal. I have no idea why, but we all thought it funny. Like other neighborhood traditions, we learned things like that from older kids.

"I told her you wrote the second half of my fire competition and aren't you happy?"

"No, you jerk. Now I have to go with you and a bunch of punk third graders to the fire department for a tour and the Boys' Club for lunch afterwards this Saturday for some kind of awards banquet or something," he snapped.

As it turned out I was the honorary captain of the fire department that weekend and Richard was made co-captain. It was quite the turmoil that week at Audubon while all the teachers figured out what to do. I still remember the winning slogan some 54 years later. "Let's have a convention to re-enlist fire prevention." I don't remember my slogan, but I probably thought at the time mine was better. Richard on the other hand could have cared less.

The Boys' Club was a safe haven for many of us from the North End. There were pool and Ping-Pong tables, wrestling mats, basketball, a small library and a craft room. Every Saturday there was a noon 'bean feed' as they called it. Each child was given two hot dogs with or without chili, one large scoop of pork and beans, onions and mustard and a soft drink. Promptly at 1 P.M. a movie was shown in the same room. The movies were in black and white and usually about a spaceman who had a propane tank on his back that made him fly around and catch bad guys. I always liked the Boys' Club because if I got in a fight, it was with kids my own age and not the usual beating by my old man.

In 1957, the Club had a "Healthiest Boy Contest." Doctors and nurses were at various stations and we had to line up and move from one testing spot to another. They asked us to cough, prodded our mouths with tongue depressors, touched us with stethoscopes, and tapped our knees with rubber hammers. We had to do some pull-ups and push-ups and then sprint a short distance. The doctors narrowed it down to about five boys. I was one of the finalists. The Director came over and touched me on my right shoulder after much discussion.

Yep, I won the first-ever Dubuque Boys' Club "Healthiest Boy Contest." I was given a check for twenty-five dollars and had my picture in the *Telegraph Herald*. The photographer had Dan McCann stand on a folding chair. He told me to remove my white T-shirt before taking the picture. I wrapped my arms around Dan's upper thighs and with a bear hug, pretended to lift him into the air. I grimaced like I was straining. The guy taking the photo really liked it when I sprinkled some water on my face as if it were sweat. It was an awesome picture in the newspaper. That was the first of many times I had my picture in the newspaper.

Kids in the neighborhood asked if it was difficult to lift that kid. I told them it was quite easy. I never did fess up to the real story. The *Telegraph Herald* dated back to times before the Civil War. Over one hundred years later I could have cared less, as I was rich.

That was until my older sister, "Raggedy Ann" asked me to loan her seven dollars and fifty cents so she could buy a new bathing suit. I gave it to her and was not re-paid until 1990. She will tell you that she paid her debt years ago. She gave me seven hundred and fifty pennies after I harassed her at a reunion.

Third grade was spectacular. I saw a girdle, was made honorary captain on the fire department, and won twenty-five dollars. The best part was becoming friends with Tom Schweikert. That was also the beginning of numerous and regular beatings by my father that would last until the 11th grade in high school. Abuse like that would never be accepted today.

Here is another song Tom Schweikert and I sang together many years ago.

*"There's a 'skeeter on my peter,
knock him off knock him off.
There's a 'skeeter on my peter, knock him off.
There's a dozen on my cousin,
can't 'ya hear the buggers buzzing.
Knock 'em off, knock 'em off, knock 'em off!"*

"The Great Contest"

That summer started my path along juvenile delinquency. Why is it that what seems like fun to a kid can be no joke to an adult? It had to be after nine at night as darkness fell over the school playground when Marty and I decided to have a contest. We each collected ten different sized rocks from the dirt outfield that wrapped around our blacktop baseball infield. We placed our piles of rocks near second base one on top of the other like an Egyptian pyramid. The contest was whoever broke the most windows won.

The prize wasn't a pack of baseball cards with a thin piece of gum inside. It wasn't a new Duncan Yo-Yo. It wasn't even a new shooter marble for our collection. It was bragging rights. We took turns and counted aloud as one window after another was smashed with direct hits from our rocks. In total we broke seventeen windows that night. The score was nine to eight. Marty won.

The next day cops, parents and kids circled Audubon. There were people in suits with badges, mothers in dresses smoking cigarettes, dirty faced kids on twelve-inch bicycles, and us. There was a group of older boys from the seventh grade smoking cigarettes and leaning up against the elm tree. Marty and I wandered over to the tree and took our approved seats on the root system far away from the tree's base. That was reserved for older kids. That was a tradition. The older you were, the closer you sat to the base of the tree.

The elm tree was at the far corner of the playground and was an area where we could hang out smoking and telling stories. Whenever the janitor, Merle would come out of the basement at Audubon we would sing to the tune of the "Death March." The song went, "Poor old Merle for the worst is yet to come, Hey!" The "Hey" was the best part. I don't know why we did that. Older kids did it and it was just tradition, same as no girls were ever allowed at the tree. That tree must have been over a hundred years old because it was taller than many homes in the North End. I like traditions.

David Nelson Nelson

"Hey, how about all the windows?" Marty said with a sudden burst of pride to the older kids. "We did that and I won."

"Holy crap." I thought as I ran fast as I could the two blocks to the back of Sacred Heart Catholic Church. Its bells were cling-clanging away to let the North End know it was noon. I hid in the stairwell of the largest Catholic Church in Dubuque and the poorest diocese of all. I knew the cops would never find me. I thought about hopping a freight train that passed through our neighborhood on its way to either Minnesota or Illinois across the Mississippi. I thought about Gordie Kilgore introducing Paul Harvey on KDTC Radio that Ma would have been listening to while eating lunch. That was her ritual that time of day. I thought about the Old Man opening his black metal lunch pail and sitting down for lunch at Celotex on the loading dock. He was a machinist and could make anything out of metal. I thought about Elsie Schroeder beating the crap out of me when we went back to school in the fall.

I walked the neighborhood until five o'clock, which was the exact time we ate supper every night like clockwork. The black sedan pulled up to 617 Lincoln Avenue. It was July 17, 1956. The temperature was 92 degrees and we all dripped sweat into our chicken salad and corn on the cob. None of us were allowed to speak at the table while eating and nothing was to ever interrupt supper. Ding-dong went the doorbell with its customary one-half second pause between each sound.

"Shit. Who the Hell could that be? It had better not be any of your friends or I'll kick the crap out of you after supper," Dad declared. None of us five kids knew who he was talking to at the time. He left the table and went out of the kitchen, past his bedroom, and into the living room.

When he was upset he would go through the list of all his kid's names, which made him even more upset. We all thought it was funny. That night though, I didn't think it funny as I knew what was about to happen. When he yelled my name again I left the table and cautiously walked into the living room. I was numb and don't remember his open hand slapping me in the right ear just before I flew away and hit the corner of my eye on the square coffee table. That slap may have contributed to my hearing loss in my right ear that I still have to this very day.

Wiping blood from the side of my face and from my ear, I remember the plain-clothes cops saying Dad had to follow them to the police station as I was going to be carded for breaking windows at the school.

Back in those days in Dubuque the police would bring juveniles into the station and card them. We were not officially booked or arrested. It was like a warning. The police actually used a recipe card and a recipe box to record information about the kid who was caught. It was frightening for a little kid and probably meant to scare the crap out of us. It worked, something worked because I was sure scared that first time.

Earlier in the day after Marty spilled the beans to the older kids at the elm tree, they ran as fast as they could to squeal on us. Marty was taken in that afternoon to the police station. His ma would not let us play together ever again as I was a bad influence on him. And I was told not to play with him ever again as he was a bad influence on me. Regardless of all that, boys will be boys. We sure had many more great times together after that.

Writing this story about windows, I wondered about the origin of the name "Peeping Tom." The name comes from the legend of Lady Godiva's naked ride through the streets of Coventry, in order to persuade her husband to alleviate the harsh taxes on the town's poor. The story goes that the townsfolk agreed not to observe Godiva as she passed by, but that Peeping Tom broke that trust and spied on her.

David Nelson Nelson

"Silent Night, Holy Night"

I have one bad memory about fourth grade at Audubon. It was Christmas time and all of us kids were filled with excitement. We participated in the annual Santa arrival at Audubon by singing carols. Every child from every grade was sprawled down the hallways, up both set of steps and some even standing near the front door. We were all waiting for Santa. The only one I didn't see was Merle, the janitor. I figured he didn't like the holiday, as he certainly didn't appear to like us kids. Good for us, I thought. Good for us.

Then we heard it. Bells were clanging and ringing louder than the sweet bells of Sacred Heart. Santa walked up the steps from the basement with a huge white bag that he could barely drag down the hall. Candies of all sorts were inside the red mesh containers with a label stapled across the top. All of us boys yelled while the girls squealed in high annoying pitches. I figured they might scare off Rudolph, Donner, and Dixon along with the other reindeer wherever they were tied. It was a great day. It was a fun day. I was so happy to be nine years old.

A girl named Patty Krutchfield reminded me sort of Howdy Doody. This was a puppet on television in 1958. She had a face full of freckles, always smiled and was just plain nice to be around. Patty's grandparents lived in Decorah, Iowa. That was about 100 miles north of Dubuque. I remember after our school Christmas party she said she was going to Decorah with her family for the holiday. I knew Decorah well as that was where my mother was raised in a Norwegian family. That is where we learned to say, "Uff-Dah," eat lefse and smell lutafisk (Yuk). I remember telling Patty to have fun and I would see her again when we returned to school.

After Christmas break the teachers were clustered in front of Miss Schroeder's office. Miss Coffee was wiping tears from her eyes with one of those cheap hankies some 5th grader had given her for Christmas a couple weeks earlier. Miss Egleholf was looking at

PALS: Part One

the floor shaking her head. Other teachers held hands and even the janitor, Merle looked down. I wondered what the heck had happened.

"Children, I have some awful news. Patty Krutchfield's mother and her baby brother were killed two weeks ago when going up to Decorah. They were at the top of a hill in their car and apparently her dad said they were almost there. When the car went down the hill, it hit a patch of ice and then slammed into a tree. Patty will not be back with us for some time because she is in the hospital, but is ok. What we want to do is collect several things for her and the rest of the family. You children bring things like food, dolls, clothes, or whatever your parents can give and we will box it up and send it to her," our teacher said.

No nine-year old boy is supposed to cry. No sixty-three year-old man is supposed to cry. People like John Wayne, Randolph Scott and our dads taught us that. Crying would be a sign of weakness. I hid behind Mrs. Cierney's garage that day after school and cried. As I write this story, I again feel pain in my heart. Screw the philosophy about crying. She was my friend.

We brought everything to school that we could find for Patty and her family. I was never taught what to say to others at times like those and to this day I regret never having said I was sorry. We went through Lutheran Confirmation together years later and I always wanted to say something but never did.

"I am so sorry, Patty." That's what I should have said.

I still think of that Christmas time tragedy whenever I hear the "Silent Night" song. The part where it says, "...mother and child" takes me back to fourth grade.

David Nelson Nelson

"Hocking"

"Run. Run. Get out of here," Darryl Wiegand yelled as he stuck a pear in my stomach. Before I knew it, there I was high tailing it out the front screen door of Ender's Grocery Store located on Rhomberg Avenue across from the Ten Pin Tap.

I always could run fast. It was my gift. And it came in quite handy that day, when before I knew it, I had stolen a pear. I didn't even like pears. Darryl was two years older and later told me he thought it was pretty funny to see me sprint across busy Rhomberg without even looking for cars or the Point Bus. He said all the older kids were rolling in laughter as I sprinted past Jazbo's house and alongside The Ten Pin Tap. I remember a blur of Audubon to my left on Johnson Street when I whizzed by.

I didn't think it was one bit funny. I sprinted straight for the one safety zone in the neighborhood. I ran right for the great elm tree. From there I could see any adult coming after me for at least two blocks. I was trying to catch my breath when I heard an odd sound.

Earlier that day my brother, Richard had fished the sloughs by the Dubuque Packing House. He had a blow out on the front tire of his bike. There he was, peddling on only one rim and I heard him coming a block away. He had three crappies hung on a stringer that were no more than four inches long. In the heat they were nearly petrified and of no use to man nor cat. He seemed like a good target. I stood and threw the pear at him. I fired it pretending to be Yogi Berra, catcher for the New York Yankees, throwing someone out at second base. I missed him by a mile. He looked to his right and sneered at me but didn't say a word.

That pear was the first, but not the last thing I stole. We used the word 'hock' for stealing. I liked that word. It also had a second definition. We would arch backwards, suck in as much air through our noses as possible, and fire a huge glob of phlegm. That was called a 'hocker' (not to be confused with a hooker). We usually

PALS: Part One

tried to hit something like a car windshield or a stop sign. The slower the oyster slid from the stop sign, the greater the admiration from other kids.

Springtime produced some of the best hockers. Winter was trying to leave, snow and ice turned to slush, and we were happy we survived another serious attempt of Nature trying to kill us the previous four months. We wore jackets and not hooded parkas. Black rubber boots were stored away and some kids were forced to wear galoshes. Consequently, some of us were sick with a cold or a runny nose. Dr. Melgard was the family doctor for most of us in the North End, and each spring he was busy visiting the numerous homes of sick children.

There were six of us standing two feet away from the stop sign alongside the Ten Pin Tap getting ready to throw slush balls at the Point Bus when one kid said, "Hey youse guys, I have a great idea! Let's see who can shoot the best hocker at the stop sign."

Just then another kid slid his tongue out like a salamander and drug it across his upper lip, pulling yellow and orange snot toward the left nostril.

One kid yelled, "Jeez, Charlie you nimrod. Why don't you wipe it on your jacket sleeve like the rest of us? You're gunna make me sick."

"My mom told me to do it that way. She said she's tired of warshing my jacket all the time," came the response.

Just then five slush balls were peppered at the two guys riding the back of a garbage truck. We all missed. A sixth slush ball had spots of yellow and orange goo on it and landed five feet away. Charlie had been sucking on his and used it to wipe his lip clean before throwing it into the street.

We stood at the pre-determined distance marked with a clean spot Charlie made with his galoshes across the slush on the sidewalk. There was pushing and shoving as we fought for a place in line. We did warm-up drills of air-sucking, throat clearing, chest heaving, and arms flailing to the sides. We were ready.

One kid after another shot little streams of steaming spit but nothing good enough for a back slap. Last to shoot was Charlie. He arched back, looked skyward, spread his arms to his sides, rattled his chest and "Pew." He hit right on the letter "o" and it never moved! There was jumping, yelling, screaming and five kids slapping Charlie on the back. When he smiled, the frozen snot on his upper lip cracked and it was the best hocker of all times. It even made a thud when it hit against the metal sign.

That night we had another cold front move in and temperatures dropped into the 20s. When I looked at the sign the next morning while on school patrol, I noticed something that has never been repeated anywhere in the North End. Apparently, Charlie's glob had slid down the sign alongside of the letter "o" yesterday. During the night it must have froze. That sign read "stpp". Yep, he changed the "o" to a "p".

I once stole a bicycle left by some kid in front of Municipal Swimming Pool. I stole a wooden plank with some other kids from inside a lumberyard. Right in front of everyone, we just slid it out from its compartment, held it over our heads and walked out the back. We used it for a diving board at a place called Flat Rock along the Mississippi River located by the lock and dam. In ninth grade I stole a bracelet from Roshek's Department Store for Mary Holdenhopper for Christmas. I stole a boat, a car, cigarettes, and many other things while growing up. Eve, in that Garden of Eden, had nothing over me!

PALS: Part One

"School Patrol"

I never went back into Ender's Store for fear of being carded again by the police. I did have to stand in front of the store when I was Captain on the Audubon School Patrol. It was supposed to be an honor to be on the Safety Patrol.

The school patrol consisted of boys and girls who wore a white strap that clung around the waist and connected diagonally across the chest. On the chest we each wore a badge of different ranks. My badge was blue for the Captain. Every day of the school year we had the honor of helping kids safely across the street as they walked to Audubon. During nice weather, it was pretty neat. I impressed all kinds of younger kids. I held the wooden pole with the sign labeled "stop" on both sides and walked right into the middle of the traffic. I held one arm out straight while commanding cars, trucks and the Point Bus to stop for me.

But one thing was certain. There was no honor to being on School Patrol in the winter. I had black rubber boots that covered my shoes that were held together with metal clasps. My feet almost froze. The thumbs of my mittens stuck to my index fingers and I had to pry them loose to grab that stinking wooden pole. The pole scratched a trail in the snow to the middle of the street where I stopped traffic. Kids could barely walk with all the coverings they wore in order to battle the minus 30 degree temperature and 25 mph winds. It took the little nimrods forever to cross the street before I could huddle out of the wind in the entrance of Ender's Grocery Store.

There was a special rule we had. If the temperature was below zero degrees all of us on patrol could have hot chocolate before we had to go to class. One particular day standing on the corner of Rhomberg Avenue and Johnson Streets, I was certain it had to be ten below zero. After forty-five minutes at my station I smelled the cocoa. I imagined the marshmallows melt in my cup that would require two small hands to hold without spilling. I saw mustaches on my friends as we giggled, pointed at one another and took our sweet time finishing our well deserved hot liquid.

As fast as my heavy black boots and one piece hooded snow suit would allow, I drug that stupid, wooden pole with a stop sign attached the two blocks back to school. It left a trail all the way in the ice and hardened snow from where I once protected humanity. Other patrol kids were arriving from Kniest Street, East 22nd Avenue, and up on Lincoln Avenue. We were so excited. I remember the pink cheeks of Christine and her frozen hair that stuck to her hood.

Sacajawea was outside in a heavy black wool coat with her head covered with a Cossack style cap and heavy woolen mittens. She stood there holding a thermometer up in the air over her right shoulder with her arm fully extended. She was focused on the mercury inside the thermometer. As I approached the schoolhouse doorway, I saw friend after friend collapse into a slump. I then understood why my friends were becoming near lifeless.

In her deep German brogue she enunciated, "Children, no hot cocoa for youse kids. It is one degree above zero. Go right to class after you put up the signs."

We did as told and I was upset the rest of the day. During recess in the gymnasium, I tried extra hard to hit somebody in the head while playing dodge ball. I missed almost every throw and didn't have my hot cocoa.

God, I hated rules.

"Ping Pong Anyone?"

The summer of 1959, Tom and I were bored as usual. This was normal for all ten-year old kids in the north end of Dubuque. Kids that age were probably also bored worldwide. We were no different. But my pal, Tom and I had made plans. We each finished making two open faced peanut butter sandwiches with Jiffy Peanut Butter. The spread was placed extra heavy on the Wonder Bread ("Helps build strong bodies in eight ways"). It had to be at least two inches thick and made it difficult to swallow. That was our tradition.

We ambled up Kniest Street toward Lincoln Avenue and took a left turn along the cyclone fence that separated the Ames and Cocker houses from Audubon. It was a warm summer day and we spotted the stump to sit on and enjoy our fare. While I don't remember the name of the family that owned Hansel, I do remember the friendly dachshund that all the kids loved. He was black with a speck of light brown on his chest and wagged his tail at all who would pet him.

One sandwich of Jiffy Peanut Butter is just enough. Two sandwiches are causes for shenanigans. Tom will say it was me who came up with the idea. But, he is slightly older than I am and probably has more dementia. So I place the blame on him. And besides - I am the one writing this story. So Hansel waddled up to us and waggled his little tail for affection. Tom couldn't stand it.

"Hey, Dave, watch this," he said as he called Hansel over to his side.

Plop. Tom placed a direct hit on the wiener dog's snout. The sandwich covered both eyes. We both laughed and howled and about fell off our seats.

"Hey, watch this," I said as Hansel was trying to throw the Wonder bread off his nose and eyes. I placed a direct hit between his shoulder blades.

That dog was trying to knock the sandwiches off his face and shoulders while us two jerks laughed. God, what idiots. Well at least Tom - because it was his idea.

"Holy crap." Tom said as he hit me in the arm. "There she is. That's the new girl who just moved in. Look at her boobs. I can see them from here."

Georgia Higgenbothem had recently moved into our neighborhood. None of us knew where she came from. None of us knew her background. None of us knew her parents. But none of us cared. All we knew was that she had huge boobs. Girls in the 1950s did not mature like girls today. If there was one in the neighborhood with boobies that stuck out, you can bet she was a friend to all little boys. And Tom and I were no different.

"Do ya know her?" I asked. "Have ya met her?"

"Heck no," he said with a devilish laugh and pushed his glasses up his nose. "How would I ever meet someone like that?"

"Ah, come on, let's go meet her. We're as good as anybody else," I said as I heard Hansel grappling with the fence behind us.

"What are we gunna say? What are we gunna do?" he asked as he pulled at my shoulder.

Nothing was going to stop me. We left Audubon and crossed Lincoln Avenue heading toward her front porch. There she was, one year younger than us and had bigger boobs than we had ever seen before. I saw her bra through the open slit between the buttons when standing on her left side. I said, "Hi, I'm Dave and this is Tom."

"Hi ya fellas," she said giggling. Do ya want to sit on the glider with me?"

This late stage in life I can't remember who shoved who first, but we both made a dash for the well-endowed siren swinging back and forth on the *glider of love*. I don't know about Tom, but I think that was the first time I fell in love – well, except for Miss Phifner. I can't remember what color eyes the new girl had. I don't remember what color hair she had. But by God, she had nice boobs.

After some simple chit chat with Tom on her left and me on her right side, she said, "Do youse guys play ping pong?"

I would have said anything at that point in time. Both of us just nodded while drool dripped from our chins. I did notice Tom's black rim glasses fogged up quite a bit.

She continued, "Do youse want to go into our garage out back by the alley and play some? Don't trip on the laundry line stick in the yard and don't look at my private clothes. My mom just finished doing some warsh and hung it out to dry."

In his excitement Tom jumped off the glider and ran smack into the support beam of her porch, because he couldn't see through his foggy glasses. He reminded me of Hansel across the street. I on the other hand was much cooler as I stood and looked up at her face when we each left the glider. She was at least four inches taller than I was, but I didn't care as her boobs were at eye level. I placed my hand into my pocket to cover my boner. Circumspectly, of course.

As Georgia and I entered the garage with Tom still behind trying to clean the fog from his lenses she said, "OK here are the rules. If youse lose a point, youse have to come over here and give me a kiss. If I lose I will come over there and give youse a kiss. Who wants to go first?"

Suddenly Tom was no longer my best friend. I grabbed the paddle and immediately hit that little ball into the wheelbarrow next to the wall. I said, "I lose. Here I come."

I had never kissed a girl before. I had watched the movies where the guy gave a peck on the cheek. But here I was going for the entire shebang. With her being so much taller I stood on my toes like a dancer in The Nut Cracker, my knees straight as any arrow Geronimo could shoot on a Saturday morning episode of Broken Arrow, my tiny back was arched, my neck was craned as far as it would go. She leaned down toward me with closed eyes, wrapped her arms around me and pulled me into her lips and her welcoming breasts.

The event seemed to last forever. I was in heaven. That event taught me the way women like it. No more than 30 seconds tops of what adults called foreplay. Tom was once again my best friend as I leaned up against the wheelbarrow and did not care who won the game.

"Run! He's Going for the Knives!"

At an early age I realized I had a gift. It was the ability to run fast. I also realized I had a temper. When one is beaten, starved, deprived of water, ignored, kicked, whipped, and verbally abused – someone else is going to pay.

My mother worked for a brief period of time until her nervous breakdowns finally got the best of her and she had to quit. When I was about five years of age, we had a babysitter named Mrs. Bradberry. She lived in an apartment behind Ender's Grocery Store. She babysat us while Ma worked. My first experience with knife throwing was with this nice old lady.

For a reason I don't remember, she pissed me off one day. I went to the drawer filled with knives and cleavers. I held the eight-inch blade overhead and threw it with all my might. It whizzed by her and stuck into the wall next to her head. My timing was perfect as Ma had another breakdown a few days later and quit her job. Mrs. Bradberry said she would never return. Sometimes in life things just work themselves out.

On another occasion, my older sister pissed me off. She was babysitting us kids while Ma and Dad were at a bar playing euchre and getting drunk. I wasn't the only child in the family with natural speed. My sister was quite the runner as well. I ran to the knife drawer and grabbed a cleaver. I was going to kill her over something. Everyone yelled, "He's going for the knife drawer!"

Two brothers ran out the front door, one crawled under the bed, and my sister ran out the back door dressed only in her pajamas. She had quite the head start. She took off like a bullet with me in tow screaming about killing her. She ran up Lincoln Avenue, turned on to Windsor Avenue, over past Sacred Heart, down Johnson Street. Now that young lady could run. I was impressed. I gave up the chase and feeling generous, allowed her to live another day. I was probably about eleven years of age.

David Nelson Nelson

Throwing knives at others gave me a sense of control over them. It gave me power I could never feel when my parents were home. It allowed me to vent extreme anxiety from the abuse I suffered. While I was never a bully to other kids, I wonder how many psychopaths or school bullies are out there seeking power from traumatic instances in their childhoods. Thankfully for all concerned, I outgrew the knife throwing after about a year or two.

Throwing knives dates back to 600 BC. The Japanese and certain North American tribes were among the first groups of people to use the throwing knife as a weapon.

"How's the Watermelon and What's That Noise?"

It was mid-July and Tom's mom and dad were gone who knows where. His sisters were also absent. Once again, we were left alone and looking for excitement. Fourth of July had come and gone. The white refrigerator was packed with food including the bottom shelf that contained a full watermelon. The summer sun was setting slowly in the western sky.

"I have an idea," I said as a smile ran across my face.

"Oh, Crap." Tom cackled as he pushed his glasses up his nose. "What now? I'm afraid to ask."

"Let's climb out on the roof over the porch through your mom and dad's bedroom window. We can take the watermelon and throw it at kids below. They will never see where the bombs came from and maybe we can plaster a few kids," I said.

"Wow. Now there's a great idea," Tom said as he hoisted the huge piece of fruit from the bottom shelf and grabbed a knife from the drawer next to it.

"Can you carry it all by yourself?" I asked.

"I think so but you'll need to get the window open and take the screen off."

Minutes later we were perched on the roof waiting for some unsuspecting kid to pedal his bike down Kniest Street or walk directly below us on the sidewalk. In the meantime we began cutting the red fruit into nine-inch pieces as the juice dripped onto the shingles beneath us.

Then we heard it. "Paladin, Paladin where do you roam? Paladin, Paladin a long way from home. A fast gun for hire is the calling card, of a man called, Paladin."

It was Fritz Schmitz pedaling his bicycle beneath us and singing the theme song to a popular western television show. As he approached the railroad tracks where they crossed East 22nd Street, we fired away.

"Wop" went the first piece against his front bike rim. "Smack" went the second one right into his shoulder. At first he wobbled and then lost his balance. The sting of the cement against his body stopped the singing. Tom and I each laid low on the roof above. We heard some cussing and through the trees saw him looking straight ahead at the hedges beneath us. He mumbled some stuff to himself, picked up his bike and never thought to look upward. The score was "Tom and I - one, Innocents – zero."

"Holy crap," Tom said as we both laughed and watched Fritz pedal up toward Huey's. "What do ya think about a car?"

"Oh, God that'd be great. Make sure it's an old guy of about 30 or so, because we don't want any of Cindy's boyfriends beating us up."

"OK, let's get the ammo ready," he said as we cut more pieces off the rind.

"Let me have two of yours cause you have a lot more than I do. Then we'll be even," I told him.

The melon pieces shook and tumbled from their perches long before we heard the train horn as it approached the intersection beneath us. Tiny rocks and small twigs danced their way off the roof and into the gutters a few feet beneath us. Two long horn blasts, one short and one long was what we heard as the Great Northern train approached. Both of us leaned forward to see if the train was a switch engine or a full load of 120 cars. It was a switch engine with three workers sitting on the front. They were about one hundred yards to our left. Neither of us spoke since we knew exactly what to do.

PALS: Part One

We were like the Bible story of David and Goliath. We had no slingshots but we had the advantage of surprise and we were loaded with ammo. It was us kids against the railroad. One after another piece of fruit was thrown as hard as we could across Kniest Street and into the unsuspecting railroad workers. We made two hits at their feet but nothing direct. One guy stood as the engine passed and shot us a bird with his left hand while he clung to the ladder with his right. We laughed and punched one another in the shoulders.

When the bells and lights stopped and the guard arm came up there was a line of several cars at the intersection. Some were going towards Sacred Heart and several were turning on to Kniest Street. We fired the last of our ammo at one car and then another. One old guy downshifted and slid on the street that was now covered with chunks of red and green slime sprinkled with black seeds. He was almost rear ended by another car just as Tom threw the last piece and hit the trailing car directly in the windshield.

"Oh shit, that's Dad," he yelled as he threw the last bomb.

All I heard was the word, "Dad" just as the melon flew from his hands. And then splat, he made a direct hit at his dad's windshield.

There he was, a former MP in the Army with a voice that would make any Jap or German prisoner melt into submission. He was screaming at the two of us on the roof. He sort of parked the car and ran two steps at a time into the house while we were climbing into the bedroom window and just finished latching the screen when he screamed, "What the hell do you two morons think you're doing?"

He never hit Tom that I know, but God he was really close that day. He told us to get out of the house and not to come back until he calmed down. We gladly obliged and ran past Tom's mother in the hallway as we headed out the door.

"Boy, is your dad ticked," I said. "My Old Man would have beaten me with the buckle end of his belt again."

"Yeah, but wasn't that great," Tom laughed as we headed towards Audubon to finish playing.

Entertainment in grades four through eight in the North End of Dubuque was probably no different than any other place in America during the 1950s and early 1960s. However, when we were bored we looked for some form of excitement and created our own fun. Sunset was the best time of day because that is when the real action started.

One late afternoon we stole a dozen eggs from Eagle's Grocery Store to throw at unsuspecting adults driving or walking past our hiding places. We rang doorbells and ran away. We peeked into teenage girl's bedroom windows. In winter we peppered the bus with snowballs. All of those activities were just little boy pranks. And one of the best pranks I pulled off was the trombone incident.

I don't remember where I ever actually found a trombone, but somehow it came into my possession by about age ten. While ringing doorbells and running away was fun, I discovered a new adventure that cracked me up with laughter.

I taught myself how to purse my lips and blow just one very loud note. During winter nights, sound would travel blocks across the frozen tundra. I put Vaseline on the mouthpiece to keep my lips from sticking to the metal. That was a trick I learned to prevent my lips from also sticking to the metal part of my sled. I hopped off the darkened sidewalk and into the five-foot high shrubs that bordered Tom's front porch. I heard a television show playing through the windows and could hear voices talking but was unable to make out what they said.

I hunkered down in the darkness and leaned against the red brick wall lining the porch. I was hidden among the bushes. With the largest breath I'd ever consumed I blew as loud as I could. The sound was a combination of an elephant, a moose and maybe even an elk. Whatever it was, it certainly got the attention of Tom, his dad and his sister, Cindy. In less than three seconds the front door flew open.

Bob yelled out, "All right you bunch of assholes. Where are ya?"

"I don't see a thing. Cindy turn off the porch light so we can see better," Tom said as he left the porch. He took up a position on the steps, and looked east toward Lincoln Ave. He was five feet away from me.

"I thought maybe I would see somebody in the street light but there's nothing," he continued.

Minutes later they closed the door and went back to their television. To this day I can't believe they didn't see the shrubs shaking as I was holding my breath and stifling my laughter. I was like a mouse staring at a coyote watching them through the hemlock shrubs.

Three minutes later I let it rip again and once again, out they ran. This time there was cussing and yelling that could have been heard four houses away. And again I was shaking with squashed laughter. "Oh God this is so funny," I thought as the trio went back inside. This time they locked the door behind them.

Some six houses away was the home of Heidi Hefferdinker. She was an old maid who needed a walker to get around. She didn't drive a car and depended on the kindness of others to help her out with errands and take her to Mass. She always watched television in the dark. As I approached her home I noticed the flicker of light and knew she was watching some television show. There were no shrubs to hide behind but I knew I could dash around the slab front porch and hide behind the corner of her house. After all, she was old and used that walker.

Another powerful blast screeched from my metal toy and I darted to the side of the house bent over laughing. A couple minutes later, the forty- watt porch light came on and I heard the door creak open. I was on my belly looking up at her as she said, "Hello, may I help youse - whoever youse are?"

I looked down the street and there again was Tom, his dad and Cindy all looking my way. I snuck through her backyard, climbed the Audubon fence and like the coward I was, left the scene. Just as I don't know where I found that trombone, I do not know what ever happened to it. But for a moment in time, I was the greatest player west of the Mississippi River.

The origin of the trombone dates back some 600 years and is from an Old English instrument called a "sacbut."

I dare you to say Fritz Schmitz and Heidi Hefferdinker ten times real fast.

"Bums and BBs"

Trains passed through our neighborhood several times a day. Two streets away from where I lived on Lincoln, there was a round house, a switchyard, and the loading site for the Pack. Throughout the entire area one could hear the sounds of trains coupling, backing up to add more cars, and the clanging of metal. There were the sounds of animals being herded off tractor-trailers at the packinghouse. Their distress calls could be heard for blocks. Diesel and oil smells permeated our ball fields, our yards, and our clothes. This coupled with the odor of dead animals from the Pack was normal.

Hobos were an everyday occurrence. There was a Bum Camp near the round house. It marked the territory between my neighborhood and the Flats. The Bums would pat down waist-high grass down into little circles. Just as we had boundaries, so did they. Each circle belonged to the present inhabitant. The bums would sleep, take a nap, eat, and drink in their allotted circles. The camp was twenty-feet away from the trains where they could easily hop on when and if they wanted to leave the area.

One time a bum came to our house asking for food. Ma gave him a couple tomatoes from our garden. As she was closing the door, he threw them on to the sidewalk and mumbled something about not liking them. I was there when Ma snipped, "Well the son's-a-bitches won't get anymore damn food from me."

I knew that instant I wouldn't get into trouble for what I had been planning. One of the kids in the neighborhood had a BB gun and we talked about shooting bums near the tracks on Garfield Avenue. In my mind, my mother had just given me the go ahead.

As we slid down the grass bank, there was only the sound of the BBs rolling inside the gun's chamber. We crawled on our stomachs like soldiers in a WWII Audie Murphy movie under the blanket of grass. We were quiet as church mice, and said not a word, but used hand signals. Neither of us knew what the invented signals meant, but we nodded in agreement when given a sign by the other.

Oftentimes, bums would sit in an open boxcar waiting for the train to depart. But on that summer day there was not a soul to be found. We figured the heck with the signals. It was fine to talk in a normal voice. We were sitting at the grassy edge where it met the bed of rocks that supported the tracks. Some one hundred-yards away, the engine sat idling. And then, we heard him, our first victim.

A drunken bum had left his own grassy bed at the camp and was staggering toward us alongside the train. Directly across from us was an open boxcar. Could we be so lucky I wondered, as the two of us slid back under cover.

"I was drunk last night, drunk the night before, and by God, I'm going to get drunk tonight like I've never been before. 'Cause when I'm drunk, I'm happy as can be 'cause I am a member of the Hummel family. Now the Hummel family is the best family that ever came over from old Germany. Yeah," the bum sang out as his staggering feet slipped on the loose rock bed.

From our sniper nest we saw his round wad of clothes attached to the end of a stick. He tossed the items into the open boxcar, put the bottle of booze into the back pocket of his bibbed overalls, and pulled himself inside the shadows of the car. Within minutes he was sitting in the car dangling his legs. He continued singing the same song, only softer.

I took the BB gun, lowered the end sites on him and fired. "Ping" it went when the BB hit the metal door handle. The guy stopped singing and looked around. His reaction reminded me of Fritz Schmitz when Tom and I had hit him with watermelon from the porch roof. I also thought of the guy looking around after I hit him in the lip with a bean from my shooter. None of my victims knew where to look for the culprit. One more shot hit him in the left chest and he rolled backwards and disappeared into the darkened

PALS: Part One

car. His cuss words were muffled by the boxcar. That guy was one mad ticked-off bum.

We each laid low and didn't move or speak. What saved us that day was probably what had saved every other boy in a situation like this, was the coupling of each car from the engine. Between the horn blasts and the train moving northward toward Minnesota, we had our escape cover. We stood up and ran as fast as we could through the grass, up the steep bank, and onto Garfield Avenue. Off in the distance I watched the bum sitting in the open car with his legs dangling. He was probably singing. "I was drunk last night, drunk the night before, and I'm going to get drunk tonight like I've never done before."

There are many versions about the origin of the term 'HOBO'. The one I like is "HOpping BOxcars" – their mode of transportation. The term "Bum" is German slang for loafer.

71

David Nelson Nelson

"Violins and Trains"

The Dubuque County School District was good to children when I was growing up. In the summer, every elementary school offered playground activities from 9-12 noon and 6-9 P.M. We were lucky; from games of four square and tetherball to horseshoe pitching contests and dodge ball, the school also offered coloring, softball and ping pong (not the "Georgia-Style"). There were numerous contests such as favorite pet tricks, sprints and relays and other games children of all ages could enjoy.

Near the end of summer camp there was a track meet held at the high school. Kids from all over Dubuque came to run, putt the shot, broad jump, and high jump. I always won first place in the fifty and seventy-five yard dashes. I remember looking for a kid from the Flats named Mean-Boy. Nobody from Audubon knew what he looked like, but we all knew his reputation. He would fight anyone regardless of size. He was definitely someone you did not want to cross. I knew he was out there that day. Somewhere in the mass of children was a kid I feared.

While stretching my legs before I ran the fifty-yard dash I heard a circle of kids screaming and yelling next to the high jump area. I ran to see what was happening along with several adults. The closer I approached I saw one smaller kid on top of a larger one swinging his arms and fists in rapid fire. The larger guy was protecting his face from blows to his nose and eyes. A coach grabbed the assailant who was still swinging and kicking in mid-air. The bigger kid was rolled into a ball rubbing his face. I froze in my tracks when I all I heard was "Mean Boy." I knew who won that fight. I retreated to safety across the field.

During the school year, the system offered music lessons and the loan of instruments at a rate of $5 per school year. I was in the third grade when I met Mr. Zwimmer who was the traveling music teacher. I didn't know one instrument from another and couldn't tell the difference between the notes of F-A-C-E and an E-G-B-D-F. Richard was in the fifth grade at the time and chose the viola. While

PALS: Part One

I didn't want to play the same, I did want to be in a similar category in case I needed his assistance. I chose to play the violin. To this day I don't know the difference between those instruments. I do remember the struggle in trying to find different notes.

Day after day I squeaked out notes that were nowhere near what they should have been. Richard swayed his right arm out to the side and moved his torso ever so gently playing perfectly. I felt like I was cutting a piece of wood with a keystone saw. I chopped, grinded and grated the catguts across the strings. No matter how much rosin I applied I stunk. I have never been a patient person. It was the third of November 1957, when the fragile instrument met the solid oak, four-drawer dresser in our upstairs bedroom.

Oh how I tried to make the notes flow like a pigeon feather as it floated to the ground off Audubon's roof. But, no, there was no way. With a slam-dunk that rivaled the camera incident in second grade, I jumped up in the air and slammed the damn thing against the edge of the dresser. I was amazed how many shards of wood went flying in all directions as the soft and hard woods met. I have no idea what my parents paid for the replacement. For some strange reason I was not beaten.

But there was one lesson I'd learned. The notes F-A-C-E for me became known as another form of music. FACE meant, "Fart At Command Everywhere." That was something I learned from Tom's dad. If you pulled my finger anytime, anyplace, I would emit a winning blast from my Fruit of the Loom underpants. I could remove the biggest of all smiles with colorless methane. Hence I became known as Fart Face - The Former Violin Player. I suppose I should have stuck with that trombone.

The sound of steel train wheels screeching to a halt on the rails would lead all of us kids to cover our ears. It was a high-pitched noise that caught everyone's attention and definitely, was not soothing to the auricle. At least four times on any given day trains might squeak, rumble or zoom through our neighborhood. The most powerful of all trains was a line led by four engines. Usually the last engine was facing backwards while the first three pulled the

120 cars towards the Mississippi River. There were times when an employee sat facing backwards in the fourth engine. He hung out the window high above us as the powerful unit raced by.

One particular day I was still suffering the beatings from the old man and was really pissed at all male adults - except Tom's dad. I walked the tracks behind the houses on Kniest Street trying to ease the pain of a sore rib and a blackened eye from the night before. I heard the sound of the barreling train coming towards me. I saw the rocks on the bed shaking loose and dropping down below the ties. The earth shook, as did my tiny chest. I was not five feet from the rail and I didn't care. Nobody liked me and I was pissed off.

There to my right was a wooden picket fence that separated the dirt backyard of Kretz's house from the railway. Intuitively, I broke off a piece of the fence. It had a pointed spear-like end and was perfect for what I had in mind. The second engine passed me by. The wind brushed me as I gathered my senses and fixed my aim on the fourth car. A worker was hanging out the window and with a gentle smile looked down at me and waved. The hell with his smile; I didn't care about anything. He was an adult and all adults were assholes that day.

I leaned back on my right leg with my right arm down at my side. And then with all my might I speared the fence piece with a direct hit right in the worker's face! I knew at that instant I was wrong and never should have hurt that fella. My side stung with pain from the recent beating. The fence piece fell back to the tracks below and was immediately chewed up by the locomotive's wheels. I felt remorse as I saw the worker disappear into the cabin.

Attacking the trains and the workers was an acceptable form of entertainment for us kids. What I did, however, crossed the line. It was in the same category as what Jake and I did.

Jake was another friend of mine whose backyard was a mere five feet from the tracks. Like all houses along the tracks, there was no grass in the backyards. Yards were filled with dirt and littered

PALS: Part One

with stones. Jake was punished the day after my spearing attack on the train worker. Jake's alcoholic father came home and was pissed about something as usual. He made Jake clean the yard. How does one clean up dirt? In order for him to go play baseball, he had to finish the chore. The two of us used leaf rakes and scraped the rocks into a pile leaving scratches in the dirt. There was a large pile of mostly rocks and a few sticks alongside the dilapidated garage. Jake eyed the coal shovel and then grabbed it from the garage I could almost see an idea forming in his head.

"Stand at the far end of the fence and let me know when the caboose is coming. I have a great idea."

I leaned against the flimsy metal fence twenty-five feet away and peered down the tracks as another train was coming in the opposite direction from the day before. I looked over to see a coal shovel full to the brim with dirt, rocks, and sticks. Jake was hiding against the side of the garage while I was the lookout. He barely heard me as I yelled the countdown... "Three, two, one, fire!"

The fella leaning out the caboose window didn't have a clue what hit him. It was a better shot than I made the day before. I heard the choking and gagging as the caboose was pulled up the tracks toward the west.

We celebrated by shoving one another and hitting each other with our fists. With the chore complete, we left to play baseball at Audubon.

The next day, he and I were lying under a junked car in the empty lot next to his house. Earlier we had ripped the outside rear view mirrors off the junker and crawled under it. Across the street there were two fellas on extension ladders painting the outside of a house. The sun was perfect, the angle was just right. Our intention was to reflect the sunlight into their faces with the mirrors. They would become disoriented and fall off the ladders.

Before we succeeded, however, our plan was interrupted. There was an official from the railroad company who walked into the back yard from the tracks. He drove a special car with train wheels and stopped behind Jake's garage. Two police officers from the Dubuque Police Department pulled their squad car into the dirt driveway off the street. From our left, came one pissed off painter screaming at us to get out from under the car.

In nothing flat I was put into the cop car for attempting to spear a railroad worker and Jake was in trouble for throwing dirt at the fella in the caboose. We were taken to Central Avenue Police Station and carded. It was my second run-in with police and the first for Jake. Our parents were called from their places of work and it seemed like hours before my dad showed up. That wooden bench in the hallway at the police station was uncomfortable and rigid, but I knew it was nothing like how uncomfortable I would be when I returned to 617 Lincoln Avenue.

"You dirty little son of a bitch!" Dad yelled as he whipped me with his belt in the basement of our house. When he missed a full contact shot, he would kick me with his steel-toed work boots.

I curled into a ball with my hands covering my head and screamed as loud as I could knowing each lash brought me closer to the end. He eventually finished and turned the light off while I lay in the dark feeling the warm blood on my back and legs dripping to the floor. I sobbed quite a bit and fell asleep there in the cold dark room.

By the time I left Audubon Elementary School, I was hardened from physical abuse. I was also a frightened and insecure child. Abuse will do that to a person. My childhood was stolen from me, I didn't trust anyone except me, and I didn't like adults (except for Tom's father, whom I adored). I used laughter and pranks to compensate my depressed inner self. That is what we did in the 1950s and 1960s. We hid our feelings.

PALS: Part One

"Life Lessons Learned"

During my years at Audubon Elementary School I learned some valuable lessons that I have carried with me to this day.

Pick Your Battles but Not Your Nose

I didn't receive any punishment from Elsie Schroeder the day of the turd incident. I did though lose some respect for her when she tried to pry that crusty booger out of her nose in front of us.

Think Critically, but Don't Be Critical of Others Less Fortunate

Just because some of those kids could not read as well as I did, I should never have judged them. Nobody knows what goes on behind closed doors.

"When ya criticize others like you're walkin' in their shoes and point a finger to blame, remember, there are three fingers pointin' back at you." (1)

Aim High for Lofty Targets and Goals

If you are shooting a bean through a bean shooter from a sewer or looking up the dress of a lady for excitement, be sure to set your goals high in order to reach your target. The same thing applies to personal goals.

Foreplay Should Last No More Than Five Seconds

Playing Ping-Pong that day taught me the true definition of foreplay. It is best to be quick. It has saved me lots of time over the years.

I Am Not as Good at Ping-Pong as An Old Man, Like When I Was as a Child

As an old man, sometimes all I can do is think of days gone by and how good I was at certain things. The older I get, the better I was.

Never Wait to Say "I'm Sorry"

"Thank your friends around you by puttin' out your hand. Shake it real firm. 'Cause this might be the last time ya see 'em here upon this land." (2)

I wish I'd known that when Patty's Mom and baby sibling were killed in the fourth grade.

You Can Wipe Dog Crap Off Your Shoes, but There Is Always a Stink

Randy running with his turd in kindergarten taught me a deeper meaning of life than just the stink of it. All negative and positive things that happened to us in our past make us who we are today. Embrace your past and appreciate who you are now. The turds of life are part of your mosaic.

Over-Prepare When Giving a Public Program

As painful as it was at the time, little did I know, the camera failure in second grade, taught me a great lesson. I am a storyteller, public speaker, and entertainer. I now over-prepare for every program I give.

I Don't Like Aluminum Foil Much

That is just one small mosaic tile in my life.

PALS: Part One

Think of Consequences When Acting Stupid

Life is like a game of chess. I think and study about a move before I make it. Pranks are fine, but picking on others is not. Picking on animals is cruel behavior.

The Garment Industry Tried to Trick Me

On the day of the great ping-pong game, I learned that the buttons on girls' blouses are on the wrong side compared to boys' shirts. One must always sit to the left of a girl to sneak a peek at boobies. I used this lesson often at Jefferson Junior High School.

(1) (2) The poems were written and previously published in David Nelson Nelson's cowboy poetry book titled, <u>The Campfire Collection of Cowpoke Poetry</u>.

David Nelson Nelson

Section II

Jefferson Junior High School

"The Melting Pot"

"Get up. It's time for school," Ma hollered as she rapped on the downstairs register with a broom handle.

Every morning, this was the way she commanded us to get out of bed. The register rapping was our alarm clock. I could hear her early morning gagging, coughing, and hacking from her cigarette smoking as I wiped the morning gunk from my eyes. I heard Gordy Kilgore giving the farm report on KDTH Radio playing below in the kitchen. I looked at my new shoes with pride, as those were the only new clothing item I had. I took my pants off the nail in the wall and turned them inside out to shake away any cockroaches. One dropped to the floor and I immediately squashed his orange guts to the vinyl floor beneath my bare heel. I rubbed the juice away on the tattered throw rug at the end of my bed. My bedroom was once a small hallway at the top of the stairs that led to other rooms that once was an apartment. The remaining rooms now belonged to my other siblings.

A couple more shakes of the trousers worn by my older brother two years before and the coast was clear. After putting on my pants and one of my brother's old shirts I snugged the thin leather belt around me and noticed a loop was missing. "Crap, I hope nobody notices this," I said out loud.

My big toe broke through the end of the sock. I knew how to roll it perfectly so it wouldn't be an issue. Finally, with excitement I put my feet into the new shoes and felt like a king. They were black in color and had a shiny bottom from having never been used. I was ready for my new adventure as a seventh grader at Jefferson Junior High School. I grabbed my spiral notebook and number two pencil from the dresser top and went downstairs. Like the other kids in our neighborhood we bought our school supplies from Walsh's Five and Dime.

It was on Tuesday, September 5th, 1961 that I first entered junior high school. I was to be twelve years old in a few weeks.

David Nelson Nelson

Audubon Elementary School was behind me and I would be following in the footsteps of my brother, who was entering the ninth grade at "Jeff," (as it was known by all who lived in the North End). My sister also went to Jeff. That year she was in the 11th grade in high school.

"Hey, Dave do you want any of these Wheaties before I start reading the box?" my brother asked as he shut the outside door after getting the home delivered gallon of milk that was on the back patio. He took the glass gallon of milk to the table and set the box of cereal in front of him and was ready to read all four sides while he ate. He would read anything put in front of him. I could have cared less about reading anything at all. It was his trick to read the *Des Moines Register* whenever it was his turn to dry dishes. He always did this seated on the throne in the bathroom after supper.

I grabbed the box and told him, "Yeah, let me get some before you hog it all."

I was one of six children that would eventually reach seven in our family. The eldest was my sister, and beneath me in age, were three younger siblings. I was relatively close with my older brother, but each of us learned to be in survival mode, because of the dysfunction in the family unit. Consequently, it was everyone for himself and for the most part, we kids were strangers sharing a house.

Each night Dad drank his Jim Beam watching television in the kitchen while Ma drank her Hamm's Beer in the living room. They did not speak much to one another. If I had to go to the kitchen for anything, my stomach turned to anxious knots. I feared my Old Man most of my life because of regular beatings that began at age eight and ended at age seventeen. Some of those whippings were justified. Others were not.

Meanwhile, in another part of town, Red McEleecse was giving the sports report on radio station KDTH as Rex's older brother yelled, "Hey get up you punky seventh grader. Do you think you can find Jeff?"

PALS: Part One

Rex's home was one block from Jeff and like me he was following in the footsteps of older siblings who had been on the honor roll each semester, members of choir, excellent athletes, and members of student council. It was expected that Rex would follow, if not excel in the path his brothers laid before him. He was the youngest of three children and his oldest brother was in the same grade as my sister at Senior High School. His other brother was in the same grade as my older brother.

Rex wore his fresh pressed pants, new button down plaid shirt, and brown shoes that matched his new belt his mother bought for him at Stampfer's Department Store. The night before, he packed his gym bag with new white shorts, T-shirts, three pair of socks still in the wrapper and white tie-up tennis shoes for physical education class. All of these were purchased from Zentner's Sporting Goods. He grabbed his gym bag, three-ring notebook containing a plastic zip lined container that housed three pencils, a pencil sharpener, one gum eraser, a protractor, one blue plastic ruler and a package of colored pencils. Out the door he shot not even stopping to have breakfast. After all, it would be just three hours until lunch, and his mother gave him the $1.50 required to buy lunch for the week in the school cafeteria.

Rex had been an excellent student at Marshall Elementary School and would have had perfect attendance had it not been for an injured dog on Rhomberg Avenue. It was the winter of fifth grade when somebody ran over a dog and instead of stopping, just kept driving.

Rex was ten-feet away next to the chain link fence that surrounded the playground. The yelping and barking startled him as he looked over to see the mutt pulling itself with its two front legs. The back legs were mangled and left a trail of blood in the ice and snow packed street. Rex ran to the rescue and was carrying the dog to the principal's office with blood squirting everywhere. The color of his parka had changed from a light brown to a deep purple. The boys were running up to him while the girls were screaming at the mangled site. The dog was screeching, thrashing, and yelping as blood squirted in all directions. One teacher who had playground

David Nelson Nelson

duty ran to help Rex. The icy sidewalk prevented her from reaching Rex in time.

That was when Rex slipped on a patch of ice himself and flung the dog into the air directly under the tires of the Point Bus as it whizzed past him. There followed an eerie silence, except for the sound of Rex's head being smacked hard on the frozen sidewalk. He lay there twitching aimlessly. Girls threw up and boys yelled a simultaneous "Ah!" The teacher didn't know what to do and apparently neither did anyone else. There was the dead dog carcass in the street and a half-dead kid flopping on the icy sidewalk like a fish out of water.

Dr. Melgard insisted Rex stay home from school for three days due to the concussion. He never missed another day of school all the way through to high school graduation. Plus, he never tried to save another dog.

"Hey what's your name?" I asked the kid who had his locker next to mine.

"What the hell is it to ya," he replied.

"Oh nothing, I was just wondering what your name is. Mine's Dave," I told him.

"It's Kosta. Kosta Nicopolas. In the Flats they call me Mean Boy," he said as he slammed the metal locker door and disappeared around the corner.

Holy Crap. I wanted to head for the toilet and throw up. Mean Boy, I thought as I swallowed the lump in my throat. I had heard about him since the third grade at Audubon. There were stories about Mean Boy being chained to a tree and attacking railroad cops that we all called Dicks. One legend was that he jumped off a railroad boxcar and hooked himself around the neck of a Dick collapsing the guy to the ground. The guy pulled his club out and hit Mean Boy five times in the back. It had not affected that third grade kid who just scampered and crawled like a daddy-long leg spider under the slow moving train and ran away among the tattered houses known as the Flats.

David Nelson Nelson

"Homeroom Number 107"

Rex, Kosta and I were in the same homeroom. Rex chose the front seat close to the teacher. I saw Kosta grab a seat in the back and so I sat next to him. This guy is going to be my friend if it kills me, I thought. He stretched out his legs, leaned back in the chair, crossed his arms and legs. He had this habit of clearing his sinus cavities on a frequent basis. He would forcefully tighten all facial muscles on the left side and almost close his left eye, and using a quick sniff he sucked in air with a rapid burst and stopped. He acted like the entire process of homeroom was boring him to death. I tried to imitate the way he sat, but was too short and would have slid out from under the desk. I didn't try to imitate whatever he was doing with his face and snot-sucking sounds.

The teacher began roll call after the bell rang. When he got to the name Nicopolas, he mispronounced it. Three times he said the name wrong and three times Kosta ignored him. Finally he said the first name out loud and Kosta mumbled, "Here, the name is Nicopolas. They call me Mean Boy."

The entire class inhaled deeply in unison and many turned to see this kid they had all only heard about. The teacher said, "Well, mister. They called me Psycho in the Army but you will call me Sir. Sit up straight and unfold those arms and legs."

Psycho continued the roll call. After the third time of calling out the name Jasper, Psycho walked over and smacked his left ear interrupting his window gazing. The student flattened and cupped his ear with his palm as the teacher asked, "What's the matter with you, are you deaf?"

"Huh?" the kid responded.

"Huh? I said are you deaf?"

"Only in my left ear. I was born that way."

PALS: Part One

"Well, well don't let it happen again," Psycho mumbled as he turned and continued with roll call.

Everyone in the class except some girl burst into laughter. Kosta had a quick and loud 'He-he-he,' type of laugh. It quit almost as soon as it started.

"All right everybody calm down," Psycho yelled.

The roll continued and then the most beautiful, angelic voice responded, "Present."

"Present? What a dork!" Kosta said under his breath while clearing his nose.

At that very moment, memories washed over me of the third grade and trying to look up Miss Phifner's dress. I leaned as far as my short legs could balance my desk. I didn't want another humiliating fall to the floor. I had to see what she looked like sitting two rows over and up front next to Rex. She was the one who didn't laugh when the kid was smacked in the ear. All thoughts of Miss Phifner escaped me at once and were replaced by the beauty of Veronica. Ah, Veronica. The name was as beautiful as her face.

She was from a different elementary school than Rex, Mean Boy, and me. Fulton was out on Central Avenue. It was home to kids from around Comisky Playground and a few of the only wealthy ones in the North End who lived "up on the hill" – as we called it. Veronica's dad owned a roofing and sheet metal business and had numerous land holdings in the Dubuque area. They were members of the country club and, unlike mothers I knew, her mother was active in social and service events in Dubuque.

Naturally I didn't know all that at the time. My animal instincts kicked in and I was on a mission. She was the most beautiful person I'd ever seen. And boy, did I try to see a show in English class later that day. I made certain I sat on her left so I could sneak a peek at her boobs. I learned a couple years before never to sit on the right side because girls' blouses are made opposite from boys' shirts.

87

Their buttons are all on the left side of the fabric. If there is to be an opening it will be on the left. That is where the phrase "left is right" comes from.

Veronica was polite and kind to me. She was that way to everyone. But what did I care about politeness. I wanted to see knockers. Her perky little boobs did not allow any button expansion (as I called it). No matter how hard I tried to peek, the window was closed. I had a terrific urge to play ping-pong for some reason.

The first time she spoke to me was when we left homeroom number 107. She had hazel eyes that ever so slightly bulged. Her blonde hair fell almost to her shoulders and she seemed to laugh at everything. I suppose it was a nervous laugh for a little girl who had hit the big-time of junior high school. To me her braces made her all the more attractive. She said, "Jeez, you guys," at least fifty times a day. Each statement was followed with a giggle.

As far as Rex was concerned, I liked him the moment we met. He had this personality that made people want to follow him. And yet, walking that day to Miss Bowlin's English class, he was a pain in the butt. He was on Veronica's right and I was on her left. He kept hogging the conversation. In a way, that may have saved me some embarrassment. I was self-conscious about being shorter than Veronica and I walked on my tiptoes to class. I probably would have had a difficult time speaking anyway because I used all my muscles and attempted to elongate from four-foot, ten-inches to five-feet.

Rex was a great listener. He would stop what he was doing or thinking about and focused both eyes on the person talking. He squinted his eyes and never interrupted the person. He was quick with a chuckle at my jokes and I had a million of them. Rex was an exceptional athlete. He could sprint and dart like a deer and jump like a grasshopper. He was about three inches taller than me and he had the ability to touch the bottom of the basketball net. That feat was impressive.

PALS: Part One

The most amazing thing happened that day at the lockers after school. I took my hidden cigarettes and matches from the top shelf and carefully put them into my top pocket and threw my books into the lower section. I slammed the door and there she was with a smile that gave me an instant erection.

"Hi, Dave" she said as she laughed a bit. "Here, I have something for you," she said and handed me a piece of paper.

And then just like that she disappeared among the other students leaving school. I unfolded the lined paper and found the best secret note I ever received in junior high school. It had two words and five numbers. It read "Call me 26842." Wow. My four-foot ten- inch height and seventy pound frame swelled into a giant-sized boy of epic proportions.

The offering of her telephone number began an almost nightly ritual where I would call her and we would talk on the phone for at least two hours. In my home we had absolutely no frills except one. Dad installed a second phone in the unheated garage. It was there I went every night after doing the dishes. During the below freezing temperatures of Iowa winters, I sat out there in that freezing garage with my parka and stocking cap on, talking with Veronica night after night.

Little did I realize that ever so slowly, she was becoming the best female friend I'd ever had. And soon, there was no more interest in peeking at her boobs. There was no more having to walk on my tiptoes to impress her. There were times I even sat on her right side in some classes.

Veronica and I covered topics like, other kids in class, who she might "like" as a boyfriend in the ninth grade, who I might "like", and a little about our home life. I was a master at stuffing my feelings and it took at least a year before I shared with her the truth: my physical abuse and loss of innocence. Sometimes we just sat and listened to one another breathe into the phone. She never judged my poverty and she never judged my sadness. She never judged anybody.

After talking on the phone (or just sitting there breathing like perverts), we would hang up and I would run down to Tom's house and to safety - anywhere away from my dad was safety to me. Tom and I had different classes at Jeff and did not see one another often in school. But every night we hung out together – usually in his basement. He had an infatuation with model cars and would construct and then paint these cars like showroom new. The first time I saw him do this wonderful trick, I wondered about his sanity.

"Hey, Dave, watch this," he said as he turned the car over with the hood, top and trunk pointing downward. And then he lit a match and set the thing on fire. He truly did. You can't make this stuff up.

"Holy crap!" I yelled and jumped off my stool to get out of the way as the black, stringy, globs of burning plastic fell to the floor and the room filled with smoke. Then just when the flame was at a pinnacle like Moses and the burning bush, he put it out by pressing the molten plastic with a spoon. After the congealed mess cooled he turned it over and presto, there was a stock car that had wrecked. There were big dents, little dents, and to us kids we pretended the driver had died in a five-car rollover crash.

We sat and admired his work as we each lit a cigarette he'd stolen from his dad earlier in that evening. Deep in that back room of his cellar, we kindled a friendship that lasted a lifetime. I would do his homework for him while he tinkered with the eventual destruction of more cars. His love of cars came in handy for me. While in the tenth grade, I didn't have a car – but Tom did. He would drive me around with some girl I wanted to impress. That is, if he didn't have a date – which he had plenty of and to me, all his dates just got in the way. There were times a girl and I were in the back seat making out, while Tom was the chauffer. He told me once he sort of liked the arrangement, because he would sneak a peek in the rear-view mirror.

PALS: Part One

"The Christmas Tree"

Being a bully is being a shallow person in my opinion. I pulled many a prank and teased many other kids as a youngster. I truly don't believe I ever intentionally bullied anyone. As a matter of fact, I remember many times sticking up for others *against* bullies. But things often go awry. There was one time that my actions were misinterpreted.

It was Christmas time in Room 107. "Psycho" allowed us to talk about decorating the room for the upcoming holiday. Everyone except Kosta volunteered to do something.

Now we all know that every town in the world has areas that are the most downtrodden. There are areas where only the truly destitute live. In Dubuque County that area was Daytonville. The area consisted of tarpaper shacks, coal burning stoves for heat, no running water and several children who slept together in the same beds or on the floor. Some floors were just plain dirt. All the kids who lived there rode the school bus the five miles or more to Jeff. One of those kids was Jasper.

Jasper was a nice enough kid. He said' "Huh?" whenever he was asked a question. From that first day in homeroom we knew he was deaf in the left ear. While he was not part of the wrestling team, he had, what is known in the sport, as cauliflower ears. Some parts were knotted and twisted and other areas had bumps where the skin should have been smooth. He told us the slight limp in his gait was from a twisted spine. He was not very intelligent and consequently was placed in the slow class.

Jasper asked if he could bring the Christmas tree as his part for the room decoration. None of us knew he planned to chop down an evergreen on the hillside behind his house. None of us knew he was not allowed to bring the four-foot tree on to the school bus. We did not know he had to walk to school. None of us knew he had no stocking cap walking the distance to Jeff when it was below zero. None of us knew he left his peanut butter sandwich at home

91

because he couldn't carry it and drag that tree to school. None of us knew or felt his excitement and anticipation to be the crowing jewel of Room 107 that day. What we did know when he came into the room fifteen minutes late was that his tree was the most pitiful tree ever witnessed by mankind.

The roadways and sidewalks had rubbed off anything green. All that was left when he limped into the room were the remnants of a small evergreen tree with sticks jutting out from the sides. Psycho laughed. I laughed. Kosta laughed. Rex laughed. Everyone except Veronica laughed. She went to the front of the room, helped Jasper lean the tree against the wall and began placing ornaments on the bare branches.

Later that day in the lunchroom I sat next to Veronica. For the first time ever, she ignored me and I was crushed. I asked what was wrong and she replied without looking at me, "I'll talk with you about it tonight. Right now just leave alone."

I felt sick wondering what I had done to breach her friendship and confidence in me. I felt like crap all the rest of the day. I did a poor job washing the supper dishes and didn't care if I would get another beating from my dad for the poor performance. I wanted and needed to talk with Veronica. I raced to the garage while putting on my parka. I dialed the number that was now etched in my brain and was out of breath when she answered.

"Hello" she said.

"Hi, Veronica, can you talk?" I asked with a nervous tone.

"You bet I want to talk. Jeez, how dare you and all the others laughed at Jasper in homeroom today. It's not bad enough that the moron teacher, Psycho slaps Jasper in the ear when he is deaf on the left side and doesn't hear the question asked of him. You people should never have treated him that way. You guys probably crushed him. I am so mad at you and your buddies, I don't want to talk tonight. You need to apologize to him. You always tell me how rough you have it. What about poor Jasper? Good-night."

PALS: Part One

The phone went dead and so did I for a moment. For that instant when my friend shunned me I was truly ashamed. For the first time in my life I put myself in someone else's shoes and felt empathy.

That was fifty years ago. Jasper died a long time back. I never did apologize – but I do now.

"Jasper, I am so sorry."

David Nelson Nelson

"Physical Education"

"All right you guys get in line and count off by fours. I don't want to hear a sound other than your number. I assume all you Jackies know how to count. Now!" Coach Udelhoff yelled at us sitting on the metal bleachers waiting to begin our first gym class.

We ran in excitement. We ran for spirit. Mostly we ran because he scared the living crap out of us twelve-year old kids. We stood next to each other along the white line that was the out of bounds marker for basketball. There we were in our shorts, shirts, socks, and shoes with varying shades of white, depending on the financial class one fit in at the time. Underneath we all wore athletic supporters or better known as jock straps. I am not certain why that was a requirement. As for me, my entire package was no bigger than a couple shelled peanuts. But we were proud. And we were becoming men. And we were frightened to death.

"All right, starting down here to my left, you will reach out and touch the boy next to you on his shoulder. That kid will step to his left and repeat. When we get to the end of the line you had better be spaced evenly apart," He barked at us. "You will all shut up immediately, stand at attention and look straight ahead. When I give the go, you will count one, two three and four. Then repeat. All right, go." His thunderous voice echoed across the gymnasium and off the cement wall behind us.

And so the count began, "One, two, three, four, five" was suddenly interrupted by his clipboard smashing to the floor and he charged up to student number "five."

Holy crap, kid. Are you deaf? Did you not hear me? Do you understand what to do?" He screamed these invectives two inches away from the trembling kid.

"I thought…" was interrupted by, "You thought my butt. Kid, I don't believe you know how to think," he continued screaming.

PALS: Part One

"Do you want to pass this class or should I put you in the Special Ed Class?"

Down the line there was a snort and then a snicker. It wasn't me, but Kosta, standing two students down from my left. Coach came running down like a quarter horse with flared nostrils, ears laid back, eyes bulging and his chest pumped out of his shirt. Again he screamed, "All right which one of you Jackies just snickered? Was it you," he asked as he shoved the biggest kid in class up against the block wall. Coach had his fist clenched and arm out to the side, and man he was ready to punch.

You could have heard the ticking of his stopwatch and there was the sound of sweat dripping on to the floor from each of us. We'd not even begun our workout.

"All right so nobody wants to fess up. So just like we did in the Army in Korea we will run. And if anybody passes out I will kick you in the butt as hard as I can. And if anybody dogs it, there will be a big payment from me," he screamed as he blew his whistle.

Thirty kids took off in different directions. Some went north. Some went south. A couple kids ran across the gym floor and out the door in fear. There was shoving, yelling and pushing. I heard Kosta say as I passed him, "Well this is a bunch of crap."

The coach's whistle blew three long blows and two short similar to the trains running through our neighborhoods as a warning when they crossed our streets. We knew to watch out for the locomotive and now we knew to watch out for coach. I think he could have been a professional glass blower in another life because, boy did his cheeks ever puff out blowing on that silver whistle with the little round wooden ball inside.

After more tripping, falling, and shoving, everyone was back in line and at attention. We started to space off in preparation for the correct count. I thought for a moment I had double vision from where that big kid hit me in the right eye with his elbow during the calamity cluster of gym class (as it came to be known). Through the

95

gym door returned the two boys who had run out moments earlier. They were twins that nobody could tell apart. When one started a sentence the other would finish it. They sounded alike and were mirror images of one another.

"Where did you two morons go?" Coach asked.

"We ran up and down the…" one replied.

"Hallway three times," the other finished.

"Oh for Christ's sake. Get in line down at the end."

As the last kid said "four" the shower bell rang and we were told we had fifteen minutes to take a shower and get dressed. Once again we were shoving, tripping and darting away from one another. We were excited; No, even more than that, we were afraid to be the last in the gym with Coach. I felt somebody behind shove me through the wooden door to the locker room and turned around to hear Kosta say, "This is bullshit."

PALS: Part One

"The Great Paint Fight"

"Didn't you Jackies hear my whistle? Get in line and count off. Today we are doing the ropes and trampoline," Coach Udelhoff screamed at us.

"One, two, three, four. One, two, three, four" was repeated over and again as we snapped our heads forward from the left as we touched our longest finger to the student next to us on his right shoulder.

It was a mere two months since the beginning of school that we had learned how to count off like Coach was taught in Boot Camp a few years earlier before he had gone off to Korea to be a part of the Artillery Division. No longer were we little morons not knowing how to stand at attention. We could run laps in a way that would have made his Drill Sargent proud. We still wore our white shoes, socks, shorts and T-Shirts that were now beginning to tighten against our bodies as we started to grow from weeks of fish sticks, sloppy joes, pizza, and chipped creamed beef over toast served every week in the school cafeteria.

The count was working its way down the line when I looked out of the corner of my one eye and I saw him running late into the gym class. He took his place at the end of the line.

"What in the holy crap do you have on?" Coach screamed as he threw his clipboard down to the recently polished basketball court and sprinted up to Danny's face. He was nose-to-nose yelling so loud that Art Henzie, the janitor could have heard him in his office down the end of the hall and through the closed doors.

Danny Sauser was a nice kid who came from the Daytonville area. He was another poor kid who was always in need of a bath and smelled like dried sweat. Danny was large for his age and many considered him fat. He was easy to pass running laps and often fell or stumbled over his own feet. We would leap over him as he tried to get up using both of his arms and legs.

"Holy Shit!" Kostas said out of the corner of his mouth while staring straight ahead. "What is he wearing?"

Snickering and snorting in a low tone so as not to have Coach hear him, Rex said, "I think he's in his underpants."

"Son, where are your clothes? Where are your gym trunks? And what the heck are you chewing? Is that gum? Are you chewing gum in my class?" Coach screamed as he shoved him back against the block wall some three feet. Danny then fell to the floor.

"Oh, no. Watch this. He's in big trouble now." Rex whispered as we all looked forward at the bleaches in front of us.

"You get your big butt up now off that floor and go sit down on those bleachers. I'll be right back," coach yelled as he tore the whistle from around his neck and threw it across the basketball floor. "The rest of you morons stand at attention."

Moments later, Coach returned with a scotch tape dispenser and The Jar. Coach kept a large jar of previously chewed gum he collected from kids over time. He told Danny to spit his gum into the jar and made him pick another from the vessel. Then Danny had to chew the used gum for forty-five seconds. After it was soft and pliable, Danny held the gum on the bridge of his nose while Coach proceeded to tape the entire wad to it. It took at least six pieces of tape to snug it tight.

"Now you get your big butt up to Lost and Found and see if you can find some gym shorts. Do you understand," he screamed as Danny ran out the double doors.

"All right. All the Ones start climbing the ropes down there, the Twos climb ropes up here. The Threes and Fours go to the trampoline," he yelled and then blew his whistle that he'd just picked up from under the hoop at the far end of the court. "I want each of you going all the way to the top of the ropes while the other kid holds it tight below. You had better touch the beam or you will flunk this class."

PALS: Part One

He approached those of us along the sides of the trampoline acting as spotters for the kid doing drills who had been taught routines earlier. There were back flips, seat drops, single and double knee drops, and kips. When finished with the five routines each student would come to a halt and dismount as taught. Each of us took turns doing our mount and dismount with the routines in between.

To my right I saw him return. Danny had a borrowed pair of gym shorts from Lost and Found. His thighs seemed to turn white below the bottom of the shorts. The stitching was stretched to the maximum. This was, however, much better than the Fruit of the Looms he was wearing fifteen minutes earlier. He had the wad of gum taped to his nose and the Bazooka's pink hue made him look like a fat Rudolph the Red Nosed Reindeer. He took his place in line as a spotter with the gum strapped to his nose for everyone to admire.

We didn't bully other students but we certainly took advantage of the weakest in the herd. And Danny was the weakest that particular day. How we behaved that day and what we did was in fun and not from the sense of being mean spirited.

For example; it was a normal and regular occurrence to ask a classmate what happened at Pearl Harbor. When the response was, "I don't know," we would hit the kid in the balls and say, "Sneak Attack!"

Another prank we would pull was to ask someone if they wanted a couple of acres. Regardless of their response we would hit them in the balls – thereby causing a couple of acres.

This caused each of us to fall the floor gasping for air and wrenching from the pain of a gonad shot. And we might have snuck up on a kid after a shower and give him "Indian Underwear" where we would pull his underpants as hard as we could up the crack of his butt. "Indian Underwear" was named such because it was like an Indian in the movies that would sneak up behind you and wipe you out. We all knew everybody was fair game. And we didn't do these pranks out of malice. We did them because we were twelve years old and we all did them because we were boys.

It was Danny's chance to mount the trampoline. A kid on either side had to help him, as he could not grab the springs and tuck and roll up on to the mat. He just bounced up and down. I didn't know if it was the tight borrowed gym shorts, the gum taped to his nose, or his obesity that made all maneuvers impossible. Regardless of which, I had an idea for a prank.

I told all the classmates acting as spotters to pull the springs real tight when he was up in the air. The whole group nodded and giggled, as we each knew what was about to happen. Danny was some ten feet in the air, we held the springs as tight as our little hands could grasp and when he hit the mat – Pew. He flew out on to the gym floor. I heard the crunching and grinding as bone hit the basketball court. There he was moaning and crying in pain. For a second I laughed and then I felt horrible. And I still do to this day.

Coach blew his whistle and screamed like a banshee. "What the heck are you doing out here on the floor? How did this happen? Are you nothing but a klutz?"

At the exact time when Coach told him to go sit on the bleaches (with his gum still intact), the Dean, Mr. Columbus Howard came into our class. He and Coach were just off to my right while another kid was doing his drills on the trampoline. I heard Mr. Howard tell Coach that Danny had walked upstairs and down the hall on the second floor to the main office where Lost and Found was located. However, he did it in his underpants and with a big wad of gum taped to his nose. The Dean slapped the Coach on the shoulder and they both laughed. I felt awful and was slow to dress after showers that day. I have never forgotten what I told others to do to him. That was just our first period of school.

Several hours later we were spread around the large wooden tables sitting on metal stools in room 222. That was our art class with Miss Courtage. The room was at the far end of the hall and there were windows along one entire wall. It gave us the vantage of watching cars pass by when we needed a diversion. It seemed there were more boys than girls in the class and as we approached our seats she scratched her dandruff-ridden hair out of habit.

"Quickly take you seats boys and girls," she said as she limped to the front of the class scratching her head. "Here Rex, your shirt is out. I will tuck it in better for you."

We all knew she was trying to cop a feel on us kids and just laughed at the old speckled pervert. We would take a touch anywhere we could get it.

"We are doing something new today and it will be such fun for each of you. I want to see what your imagination will capture on paper as we begin the new section on watercolors. Now you will see," she said as she was interrupted by loud chatter.

She clapped her hands together and shook more flakes of skin onto the table beside her. "All right now. Everyone be quiet while I explain today's assignment. Each of you has a jar filled with water at your table. There are paints before you. Everybody take a sheet of paper from the center of the table and dip your brushes into the paint. Let's see who can create the best design in the next forty minutes."

"Now, Mr. Nicopolas, did you hear me? Be quiet and quit disturbing Rex. I want to see how well each of you can do."

"Yeah, yeah, yeah." I heard Kosta say as he plopped his brush deep into the quart jar filled with water.

It wasn't ten minutes into the project that I had an idea. I mixed the most beautiful blue with the ugliest orange and tapped Rex on his right shoulder.

"Hey," I said, as I flicked the paint all over his face and it ran down toward his chin.

Laughing aloud, Rex said, "Holy crap. Take that Kosta."

Kosta joined in on the fun and fired some green paint onto Dave Higgen.

And so we were off. Higgen fired at Richardson. Richardson fired a brush full at me. I smeared some paint on Kosta's face with my brush. Rex turned around and nailed Schweikert with some pink that covered his glasses. Before we knew it there were boys across the room nailing one another with paint from their paintbrushes. The wimpy girls screamed in terror and in fear of getting their hair or dresses covered in paint.

I remember Miss Courtade running out the door scratching her hair with the wooden part of a new brush yelling for help. It was so exciting. I grabbed my friend, Rex by the arm and said, "Follow me."

In nothing flat I opened the double doors of the storage cabinets under the counter tops along the windows. We were short enough to fit perfectly into the storage bins. We closed the doors after us. We held the inside of the doors snug as we heard Mr. McMurphy from shop class, Mr. Howard and Mr. Cheswick, from mechanical drawing, all joining in to help Miss Courtade gain control.

There was yelling, screaming, and girls crying as paint and water were flung everywhere. All the boys seemed to look like Sioux Indians on the warpath. Rex and I giggled at each other in the dark and held our fingers to our lips motioning for quiet. The darkness was interrupted by Mr. Howard bellowing, "Get out of there now!"

"You, Rex of all people," he screamed. "You, the president of your class. I am ashamed of you."

We were caught. Miss Courtage didn't know who started the Great Paint Fight (as it was to become known years later) but there were six of us hauled into Principal Orser's office. There was Higgen who had his big lower lip covered in black, Kosta with blue eyebrows like a cheap street walker, Danny with yellow dripping off his Bazooka bubblegum, Schweikert's natural black hair was now green, and he had a pink mustache. Rex had a blue and orange chin like he had been chewing cheap tobacco, and me with all the primary colors from my forehead to my throat. Mr. McMurphy led the way telling us to shut up, and just be quiet. Mr. Cheswick was in the middle of us, followed by Miss Courtade scratching and limping at the end of the line.

We were made to stand in single file while the three teachers went into the principal's office yelling about what had happened. I looked to my right and saw the Lost and Found box where Danny had arrived several periods before, to find gym shorts. Principal Orser's office door opened we were told to enter single file.

There we were, standing in a semi-circle in front of his desk. He was so irate he could not even look up. In front of him on plain paper were all of our names. It was execution time, I thought.

I was ready to blame it all on Rex when the silence was broken. "All I want to hear is guilty or not guilty," Principal Orser said, as he continued looking at the names in front of him.

"Schweikert?"

"Guilty."

"Higgen?"

"Guilty."

"Nicopolas?"

"Guilty."

"Rex?"

"Guilty."

"Nelson?"

"Guilty."

"Danny?"

"Guilty" He said in a nasal twang as if his nose was stopped up.

For the first time Mr. Orser looked up and asked, "Son, what is that on your nose?"

"It's bubblegum. Coach Udelhoff made me put it on at first period today cause I was chewing it in class. He told me to wear it all day."

"I want you to throw that into this waste basket right now! Get that off your nose," he demanded.

Danny pried the goo from his nose after nearly six hours of the clumpy mess being stuck to his nasal passage. He dropped the wad into the metal wastebasket with a loud thump.

"All right you have all been found guilty of disrupting Miss Courtade's class and I sentence each of you to seven after-school eighth periods. This will begin today. Now, get out of here."

I was not saddened because Danny wore the gum all day. I was not saddened to be sentenced to after-school detention. I was sad because I didn't have the chance to blame Rex.

Chewing gum dates back to the ancient Greeks. The citizens back then chewed mastiche made from the resin of the mastic tree. North American Indians chewed the sap from the spruce tree. Mayans chewed sap from the sapodilla tree. On December 28, 1869, William Finley Semple patented chewing gum – US Patent number 98,304.

"Linwood Cemetery, Pop, Marilyn"

The school year of 1961-1962 was a great year. I set a couple records in track in the sprints. I spent almost every evening talking, listening, and sometimes just breathing on the phone with my friend, Veronica. When I wasn't on the phone with her, I was in the comfort and safety of Tom's house. It was there I could be me.

I wrestled at the seventy-pound weight class and was elected to the student council. I was active with vocal music and was still ringing doorbells, stealing cigarettes, and throwing missiles at the railroad workers. Christmas of 1961 I stole a bracelet for my girlfriend Mary Lou, from Roshek's Department Store. I had no money and was bound and determined to make her mine forever. After giving it to her, I just knew she would let me touch her boobs. But three days after we returned to school from the holiday, she broke up with me. What a creep. If I'd been caught stealing that bracelet, I could have been carded for the third time at the police station. Veronica had warned me earlier that Mary Lou was no good for me because she had a new boyfriend every month.

That next summer Tom and a Catholic friend of ours named Hank and I hung out quite a bit. Hank went to a different school. It was a hot August night in 1962 when we camped out in Hank's backyard lying on top of sleeping bags. My two friends pointed to the North Star, to Orion, and to the Big Dipper. I could never see what others saw in the night skies so I just pretended to enjoy the evening show. We lay awake for hours waiting for all the adults to go to sleep so we could begin our night prowling. All that separated us from freedom was the seven-foot high fence lining the Audubon boundary. When we saw the last of the house lights go out we knew Hank's mom had gone to sleep. Just to be certain, we lay there for another 30 minutes sharing stories about The Lone Ranger, Superman and shooting bums over on Garfield Avenue with our BB guns.

It must have been past midnight when we scaled the fence like a bunch of Marines from WW II. We each picked our climbing spots and crept to the top of the fence with ease like a black bear climbing trees. This maneuver had been done a thousand times in our youth. Tom took the exact spot where earlier he plopped a peanut butter sandwich on the nose of Hansel, the wiener dog. We jumped from the top of the fence and landed in the rain ditch on the other side. Feeling exuberant, we whispered in excitement and celebrated our freedom.

"Let's go around the corner and head down Kniest Street and ring some doorbells," Hank suggested.

"Oh sure, get *my* butt in trouble," Tom responded. "What if the old man is still awake?"

"OK, how about we head up Windsor Avenue and see what we can get into? We haven't been up there in a long time," I suggested.

Hank spoke up. "Hey, let's go to Linwood Cemetery. It's a full moon and we could scare the crap out of each other. Maybe we could play hide and seek."

"Oh, God that'll be great," Tom said, pushing his glasses up on his nose, as we all started to sing.

"Born on a mountaintop in Tennessee, killed a bear when he was just three, hung his Ma from a Christmas tree, and now he's in the penitentiary. Davy, Davy Crockett, king of the wild frontier."

Some thirty minutes later we climbed the limestone wall and fell into one of the oldest cemeteries in Dubuque County. There was a slight wind and a full moon that night. Over a century and a half ago, the bereaved had placed a series of short headstones near the front gate. And on this night, the bright moonlight cast long shadows across the spooky sight. We walked up the roadway toward the crest of the hill and saw seven-foot high marble monuments pointed on the top that signified someone with lots of money from long ago had once been alive in our town. But now they were all equal, from the once high and mighty rich people to the poor German immigrants rotted down below. The winds blew the evergreen treetops, while off in the distant we heard a dog howling and a train heading north along the Mississippi toward Minnesota. The singing quieted down and we walked at a slower pace.

"OK, who's going to be 'it'?" I asked.

Tom was glad to be the first and told us that we had one minute to go hide. He turned, leaned against a monument, closed his eyes, and started to count. Screeching and yelling at first to see if we could wake the dead, Hank and I raced off in different directions. I hurdled headstones off to the left while Hank ran right towards the fence line. Some fifty-yards ahead of me I saw it, the greatest hiding place of all. It was a recently dug grave with a tarp over the top.

"Holy crap." I thought as I pulled back the black plastic tarp covering the hole. They'll never find me here. The sides of the earth were soft and easy to kick holes into the walls for foot placement. Tomorrow there would be a casket but tonight this resting place was mine. I clung to the side of the pit and waited. I heard Tom off in the distance yelling for us after he stopped counting. I imagined shapes from the dead floating near me, and the sound of falling dirt into the pit made me breathe harder and faster. I clung to the grass roots at the top and felt the plastic crinkle of the tarp covering my head. I looked left and right trying to spot Hank and Tom. I imagined they could hear me breathing, as each breath seemed to move the plastic even more. I refused to be frightened or at least that's what I said from my perch hoping not to fall six feet below. I smiled to myself thinking how funny it would be if the grave diggers found me in the morning down in the hole. Or even better, crawl up and out and simply say "howdy" to the grieving family sitting next to the grave.

"Where do you suppose that nimrod went?" Tom asked as he and Hank came walking up the pathway.

"I don't know. And I can't believe you found me so quick," Hank complained.

"Let's be real quiet in case he hears us coming," Tom whispered.

"Shit. Look over there. It's a new grave for tomorrow."

Pretty scary." Hank said as he pointed directly at me hiding under the tarp in the moonlight. Neither of them saw me.

I smiled to myself as they planned a strategy to locate and then scare the crap out of me. I could wait no longer. From the grave below, I gave out with a shriek that caused both of them to yell in fright and run in different directions. I crawled out of the hole and lay on my back laughing at my two wimpy friends. After a bit I was cussed out but declared the winner for the night.

We shoved, poked and laughed at one another as we walked the path back to the front entrance of Linwood. The noises of boyhood echoed off the granite reflectors. Little did I know, that some 25 years later I would return to this spot to bury my dad followed a few years later with the death of Ma. And then my younger brother, Charles would also be put to rest not far from this very site.

It was nearing three or four in the morning when we jumped the rock wall and crossed the street by Christensen's Greenhouse heading back to our own familiar turf down on East 22nd Street.

"Look," Tom yelled. "Do you guys see what I see? Look at that bakery truck down by The Milk House."

"Are you thinking what I'm thinking?" I asked.

"Let's wait till he leaves and make a dash for it in case there are any workers there," Hank said.

What we had witnessed was the delivery of three commercial sized boxes of donuts from the Sunbeam Bakery located in the south end of town by the East Dubuque, Illinois Bridge. In the middle of the night, the driver dropped them off by the back doors of every business that had accounts with the bakery. There must have been five or six-dozen donuts of all flavors and shapes in the three boxes that measured three-foot wide and four-foot long. There were bear claws, raspberry-filled, plain, sugar coated, cream filled, donut holes, long johns covered with chocolate and my favorite - dark chocolate covered with sprinkles on top.

"Let's wait to see if anybody comes out," Tom said. "I see a light there by the back."

"Bullcrap, I'm going for it. Let's go." I yelled as I sprinted across the street at least 20 yards ahead of the other two. We pulled open the top of the nearest box and six small hands grabbed everything we could find. The style or flavor didn't matter, not one little bit. One would have thought we hadn't eaten in days. As a matter of fact, I probably had not eaten, as I always seemed to go to bed hungry. There was laughter, there was shoving, and there was pure adrenaline. We must have just stolen at least two-dozen donuts and ran down East 24th Street towards Sacred Heart and Comisky Park. We sat leaning against a huge oak tree on the corner of Prince Street and East 24th, gobbling our goodies to our heart's content.

Tom had chocolate, banana cream and sprinkles all over his face. Hank's face was plastered with both regular and powdered sugar. Me, I couldn't tell what my face was like, but I shoved that long john down my throat where only the rounded end stuck out.

I had a sudden idea. "Hey, do you guys want to go back up the hill and steal some milk if they delivered it yet?"

"No, but I have a better idea. Let's go to the laundromat and steal a pop." Hank said.

"Well now how the heck are we gunna do that? We don't have a church key and a straw," Tom said.
"Oh yeah," Hank said as he reached into his back pocket. "Look at this." He pulled a bottle opener and a flattened, bent-in-half straw from the back of his left shorts pocket.

"What in the Sam Hell are you doing carrying that stuff with you?" I asked.

Wiping the sugar from his mouth he responded, "You just never know when these things will come in handy."

A "church key" back in the 50s and 60s was a bottle opener on one end and a can opener on the other. Pop (soda or Coke - depending where you grew up in America), was dispensed in coolers that sat upright. There was a metal maze that the purchaser had to maneuver the bottle through after inserting the nickel. At the end, a flap opened and the bottle was lifted up and out.

We ran with a sugar high the entire one-mile distance to the laundromat on Rhomberg Avenue. As usual I set the pace for the other two slow pokes behind. I pretended running before a crowd of thousands and every so often I slowed down as I crossed the imaginary finish line and raised my arms to the roar of the crowd. Then it was off to another event in track & field. This time it was the 220-yard dash. My mind was perfect that night. My dad couldn't hurt me and nobody would beat me in the races. I was in control and I was at peace in my heart.

"Oh, no. I get to go first because I was the first to get here," I insisted as we argued who would be hoisted up by the other two and held on top of the pop dispenser.

Hank looked pissed. "Bull Crap. I got the church key and the straw. Youse two have to hold me cause I'm going first."

Reason gave way to ego and Tom held Hank's left foot while I cupped his right one with my interlaced fingers. We hoisted him to the top and he immediately grabbed the side of the cooler with his left hand. Bending over into the machine we heard the fizzle of spilling pop from the bottle when he removed the cap. He sucked its contents dry in no time, gave out a belch and hopped down from his perch. One by one we emptied bottles of pop, one after the other in great gulps.

PALS: Part One

That type of pop dispenser was not around long. It was replaced by the upright bottle dispenser, which prevented theft. I would like to think that in some small way we had a part in changing America's refreshment industry. For at least two years we never paid for any drinks.

"We'd better get going home and hop the fence or we'll get caught by your ma," Tom said.

We all agreed and this time walked back up Lincoln Avenue from one streetlight to another eventually turning into Audubon and climbing the fence. There was not much to be said, as we were tired and ready to hit the hay. That was August 5, 1962.

"Hey boys. Hey boys. Wake up. I just heard something awful on the radio." Hank's mom said, standing over us in the backyard at about 9A.M.

"Marilyn Monroe died last night. Isn't that awful?"

And indeed it was awful to us 13 year-old kids. Who would we think of in that special way, now that she was gone? I imagine every boy our age thought of her at least twice a day when we were not playing baseball, shooting hoops or in our cases stealing something. Naturally we thought of her every night as well before drifting off to sleep. Life after Marilyn died seemed like it was never the same. Nothing again was the same. That was the last time I ever played with Hank. He continued going to the Catholic school and things just changed. Life moved on for all of us.

Supposedly, this is the origin of the term "graveyard shift." Apparently, in the 19th Century some folks were buried while still alive. A device was placed inside the casket that would allow the person to ring a bell if he woke while buried. Workers sat at the grave during the night to listen for the bell. I wonder how they even realized a living person was buried in the first place? Imagine

David Nelson Nelson

the physician waking up in the middle of the night with an idea and he runs to the grave with a shovel. I like folklore. It legalizes lying.

PALS: Part One

"Twice a Day Confessions"

Jim Faber was a Catholic who was asked to leave Holy Trinity School because he was caught smoking one too many times. It didn't help that the Head Nun had it in for him. He put in more hours after school than Kosta, Rex, Tom or me combined. That nun made him wash the blackboards, slap the chalk from erasers, polish the wood floors, and sweep the sidewalk. He never knew what ticked her off so much, but she most certainly did not like him.

We knew this kid long before he arrived at Jefferson. Reputations grew quickly and faster than Mickey Mantle sprinting for second base. Any insurrection against authority mushroomed the perpetrator into stardom. The legend goes that Jim walked into the office at Holy Trinity one morning and was greeted by the secretary saying, "Hello, Jim. What can I do for you? Why are your cheeks all puffed out?"

With a huge explosion from his small lungs and tightened abdominal muscles he let go with a puff of smoke that nearly filled the area behind the counter. The secretary was bent over wiping her eyes and gagging for help. Jim leaned his left elbow up on the counter, propped his head against his hand and continued puffing away on his Marlboro like a James Cagney character in some crime movie. The ashes grew, as did the suspense.

The head nun, Sister Mary Louise came running out of her office with an oak pointer with a black rubber tip on the end. She shoved the choking secretary against the file cabinets almost knocking her to the floor and screamed at her to call Father Ralph immediately. Sister never turned Jim around to hit his backside. She whaled away at any body part that got in the way of the stick. She beat him with all her strength. Jim continued puffing away and spun his backside toward her. She continued pounding away until Father Ralph ran into the room and grabbed her right arm in mid-swing.

"What in God's name is going on here," he demanded.

"This heathen came into the office smoking. Yes, he walked right in here with that cigarette. I want him expelled. Why I want him excommunicated. The Holy Father in Rome needs to hear about this!" she screamed at the priest.

"All right everybody calm down. Margaret, I want you to call Jim's mother and get her here now. Sister, you go somewhere and collect your composure. I suggest you go to chapel and pray for forgiveness for what you did to Jim."

She fiddled with her rosary beads, squinted her eyes at Jim, and ground her teeth as she stormed out the door toward the chapel. She didn't see the wink Jim gave her. If she had, the Holy Father in Rome might indeed have become involved in a murder case.

It seems earlier that day Jim had served morning mass with Father Ralph at ten minutes after seven before school began. All Catholic school kids had to attend mass every day and attend confession. It was the third period when Jim's class went to the eleven o'clock mass. Sister Mary Louise noticed he did not go to confession and demanded he do so. He told her about confessing earlier before school when he served mass. She twisted his left ear like ringing out a washcloth and demanded he go. He followed her orders.

"Bless me, Father for I have sinned. It has been four hours since my last confession," he said.

"What? Why are you here, my son?" Father Ralph asked.

"Sister Mary Louise made me."

"Well then, have you sinned in the last four hours?"

"Yes, Father I had impure thoughts about Sherry Kretchmeyer an hour ago."

"So have I my son, say two Hail Mary's and one Our Father."

PALS: Part One

The more Jim thought about having to confess twice in one day and especially spill the beans about Sherry Kretchmeyer, the more ticked off he became. And so it was that he went to his locker, took out a hidden Marlboro and entered the office. It was the last time he smoked in that school. It was the last time he *went* to that school.

By the time Jim arrived at Jefferson the next day we all knew about the event. He was already a minor god in our eyes. Kosta and I talked about him in homeroom. We had a new smoking buddy, but more importantly, Jim was an immediate friend as he too despised authority.

Jim was the second biggest kid in our class behind Alan Meade who wrestled heavy weight and was our fullback on the football team. Jim was the first person I'd ever met who could talk without moving his upper lip much at all. That intrigued me and I also like the way he told jokes and stories each time we were together. I liked to make others laugh and so did Jim. He was a prankster who had naturally good looks, stood a head above all of us, and had bulging muscles from lifting weights with his older brother. He was an immediate hit with the girls. To seal our friendship, he appreciated my tip about sitting to the left side of the girls to sneak a peek at their boobs. Jim and I were immediate friends. And still are to this day.

David Nelson Nelson

"Baking Bulbs"

"So did you hear what Jim did today in homeroom?" Veronica asked when I called her that Thursday evening.

"No, I didn't see him today. What'd he do now?"

"Well jeez, you guys are always up to something," she said with a giggle. "I heard the whole story from Sharon, while we were dressing after physical education. It seems…"

"I don't care about him, tell me about the girl's locker room," I interrupted.

"Will you shut up? Jeez, I swear that's all you think about. Anyway, if I may be allowed to continue, you know those Frigidaire ovens they have in the home economics room? Jim removed the racks and re-positioned them. Then he propped open every oven door up against the racks and the inside lights automatically came on. When Miss Maus came in she was upset that somebody played with her ovens. Even before roll call was taken she yelled at the class about the doors being left open. Using both arms she slammed the two oven doors shut. The racks smashed into the light bulbs and there was glass everywhere."

"Oh, God I wish I could have seen that one. That was great. How come I never heard about it?"

She laughed. "Jeez, you stick with me and I will keep you up to date."

"So tell me more about the shower room."

"No, I told you before how frightening and embarrassing it is to have to shower with everyone in the open. Don't even ask who, but there are some girls who have no chest at all and still wear undershirts. The worst part is when Miss Wolfkin stands there watching all of us. She checks off her list on the clipboard to make sure we showered. I hate that class. It is a nightmare."

In the early 1960's, the only sports for girls in high school were cheerleading, tennis, and golf. There was just cheerleading for girls in junior high. In gym class they had to perform calisthenics, climb ropes attached to the gym ceiling, do push-ups, chin-ups, and run laps, just like the boys. Physical education was held twice a week.

The boys had gym twice a week as well, and then three times a week we had either shop class or mechanical drawing. I never liked either one of those classes for some reason. I do remember Kosta, Rex, and I giggling when the teacher told us about a file used for trimming wood called a bastard. They laughed out loud when I said it reminded me of my old man. The next day coach made us run laps in gym class for disturbing the shop class the day before. What a bastard.

We learned different sports in physical education. One time we went to a bowling alley and learned how to bowl. We used real arrows when being taught archery. We learned wrestling, basketball, and football. Kosta and I were the only ones in our gang who wrestled. All of us played football and ran on the track team. Rex and Jim played on the basketball team.

"So did you tell these guys what you did just before we came down here for lunch," Jim asked Rex.

"No and I'm not going to either," he quipped.

"All right, what did you do? You can tell us. We won't tell anybody," Kosta said, sucking air into his left nostril.

"Oh yeah, Nelson will spill the beans to Veronica tonight on the phone," he snapped back.

"No, no, I promise," I lied.

"All right, I had to model the new basketball uniforms for the principal."

We all laughed and Kosta spit some milk on the table. We imitated our version of Rex on display with the new uniform. There was head tilting, arms flaring to the sides, and I stood and gyrated my hips. Other kids looked over from the far table to see what was happening. Coach slapped Kosta on the back of his head and told him to clean up the spilled milk.

It was the very next week when Rex had to lead the basketball team on to the court in front of the PTA. The emphasis of that meeting was physical education. The basketball team was showing the community their new uniforms. Rex was captain of the team and came out first.

We were there to demonstrate trampoline moves, rope climbing, wrestling moves and shoot some baskets. Some of us were chosen because of our abilities. Others were chosen because their parents were PTA officers.

Rex and I were about the same weight so we were teamed up against each other to wrestle. While he was good in basketball, my best sports were track and wrestling. That night in the locker room, he asked me if I could go easy on him and not humiliate him before all the parents and teachers. He asked if we could have a tie. I agreed. I was as big a liar then as I am today. I pinned him in about forty-five seconds. The last I heard as he walked off the mat was "bastard."

Male coaches also taught certain classes like math or science. By the end of the 1960s these men received an extra $5,000 more than their female counterparts simply because they were men. They were considered the breadwinners and thus the difference in pay.

PALS: Part One

In 1961, the cost of a gallon of gas was 25 cents, a loaf of bread was 21 cents, and a new car cost $2,275. Oh for the good old days.

David Nelson Nelson

"Boners, Farts and Peeing Contests"

Veronica and I covered everything possible for kids our age during our ritual phone conversations. No matter how hard she tried, she could never teach me feelings and how to share them. After all, I came from the North End and was a member of a large, poor family where physical abuse was a daily occurrence. Just like Mean Boy, I had to battle for respect and survival.

"Jeez, you guys are all disgusting," she said to me one night as we talked on the phone.

"What? What did I do now? Trust me I'm innocent," I told her and smiled into the phone.

She giggled, "Dave, you have never been innocent in your entire life. I saw you, Rex, Jim, Kosta, and Tom all laughing at the locker when Jim bent down and squatted with his behind against his locker. I know what he did. And Rex, of all people. He is our class president and you guys are corrupting him. I suppose next you will be trying to light them like my older brother and his friends do here at the house. What is it with you guys?"

I never told her that lighting farts was something Tom and I had mastered years before. We learned the art from his dad. We three had it choreographed to the point that when one composer had the urge for a symphonic release, another would throw him a lighter while the third would turn off all the lights. K-Boom! There was the most beautiful blue and orange flame that could bolt to the floor in a nano-second. This of course, was followed by great laughter and congratulations all around.

I suppose the art of fart lighting began by mistake when a Cro-Magnon Man bent over next to his fire and he spewed out some methane after eating a saber-tooth tiger. Can't you picture the other fellas cracking up? I can.

Now the incident Veronica referred to that evening was indeed true. We were always looking for new sounds. Each of us tried to find new and disgusting places to press our rumps against to create melodies never before heard. We were the methane maestros. Earlier that day we were served sloppy joes and mixed vegetables. The juice from the vegetables ran into our burgers filled with the gas-bearing beef. We didn't care, as this was our favorite cafeteria food. The first time we were introduced to fish sticks was at Jefferson. These created only sixteenth notes of fart blurps. They did nothing to activate the ilium, duodenum, or jejunum.

All of us were hanging around Jim's locker when his gaseous rumbles started. With great anticipation we all leaned forward as he bent down and pressed his butt against the locker door. He held the door with his left arm, tightened his stomach, and let rip a seven second explosion that sounded like the first chair in the trombone section of a band. It was a perfect G Flat. We laughed and slapped each other.

There are all types of farts and us kids tried to re-invent as many as we could. The best or worst fart – depending on your religious beliefs and political persuasion, is a combination of hard-boiled eggs and beer. That combination was left for the adults around us, as we did not drink beer – obviously. We saved that combination for years later as adults. There are popcorn farts, silent – but deadly, farts, odorless farts, and farts yet to be invented. A fart could be (and often was) a weapon. We would have a friend pull our finger only to explode and he would fall to the ground as if he'd been shot. We'd point our index finger, thumb pointing upwards, and remaining three fingers cupped into our palm. This was our pistol that we would shoot from a distance also causing someone to hit the ground. In case we ate fish sticks we would put a Band-Aid on the end of our index finger and that was our "silencer" due to the quiet, popping sound. Our prey still had to fall. That was the rule.

Farts could also be entertaining in another way. There was nothing that brought silent laughter more to a boy than to blame someone else for his own explosion. Jim was the absolute master at this game. In eighth grade civics class with "Popeye" Harmon, Jim let one rip against the hard oak seat. He jumped into the air, pointed his finger at Kosta and yelled, "Jeez, Kosta you're awful."

The entire class erupted in laughter. It did no good for Kosta to deny because mob mentality set in and everyone believed Jim. Kosta was escorted again to the Dean for punishment. The only thing he did wrong was to fall asleep in class and then to be awoken by the false accusation. After detention that day he went on the prowl looking for Jim who by then was long gone. All was forgotten by the next day.

Another naturally occurring event in boys aged eleven through about fifteen was the instantaneous erection. We never knew what caused it. It could appear from nowhere. We would brag about balancing our books on the little fella as we walked the halls of Jefferson. It's amazing how our egos swelled our imaginations. In reality, I would have been lucky to balance one of those removable erasers that can be placed over the end of a pencil. To hear me tell it, I could balance my geography and science books on it while clapping my hands and singing *Camp Town Races*.

Mr. Schultz was a former drill instructor in the Marines. He was a WWII veteran with a flat-top haircut and a tattoo on his left forearm. His deep voice sounded like he was talking from the bottom of an empty, fifty-gallon barrel. It rumbled and reverberated into the hallway every time he spoke. He was our science teacher. That was the only class where Kosta sat up straight, unfolded his arms, and kept his feet under his desk. That was also the only class where Kosta did not sleep.

"Hey, Rex. Look at this," I whispered, as I spread my legs and showed him my boner.

His laughter got me in trouble. Imagine that. Mr. Schultz would never have thought Rex would be the cause of such an interruption. The bastard.

"Nelson, come up here and draw the parts of a cell on the blackboard," he bellowed.

PALS: Part One

There was total silence. I could not move. My mind defied all thoughts of getting the crap kicked out of me by this Marine. All I could think of was getting that stiffened pecker to drop. All guys know that, indeed what women have said for centuries is true. Our peckers have a mind of their own. And this was indeed true that October morning in 1962.

I don't know if it was the cool Iowa morning and the little thing just woke up like a cold-back horse that had not been ridden in a while. It might have just wanted to poke its head out and see what was happening. Whichever, I was in trouble because it would not go away. Now at age 63, I would kill for that reaction.

"Did you hear me?" Mr. Schultz yelled. "Get up here now. Better yet, come up here and stand at attention in the corner. Now."

Rex suppressed a laugh, sputtering like an old water faucet.

By this time I placed my right hand into my pocket to hide it and try to reduce its rigidness. All that did was to create true torque and lifted my heels up from the floor and made me walk on my tiptoes to the front corner. While that may not be true, it was the affectation my mind used at the time. Rex was snickering and everyone else wondered what was happening. I knew the "position." I had to do it many times at home. I stood two feet from the corner, hands behind my back, leaned forward so the only support I had was my forehead. In this case, little did anyone know I had additional support. It was the first-ever two-point vertical support maneuver created by a kid. Yep, one was my head and the other my pecker. Now that may not be true – but one day it could be.

"Hey, what are you doing in detention?" Kosta asked.

"Remember in science class today?" I answered. "What about you? What did you do?"

"Crap, I got caught sleeping again. Hey, here comes Jim. We can have a party." Kosta said sucking air into his left nostril.

Naturally the teacher overheard us. "Quiet you two or you both will be back here again tomorrow."

"Farting again?" I whispered to Jim.

"Yeah, but it was well worth it. It was loud and stinky."

"Sloppy Joes every time." Kosta grinned.

We all pretended to read our books and finished our detention for the day. As an old man I am still tempted to "cut one loose." But at my age I'm afraid of the "Dreaded Surprise," a fart with a lump in it. All I can do is look back at those grand days of playing music with our rumps. Those torque producing erections that would last for hours are long behind me as a faded memory. They have faded away like tears in the rain.

Now, back to the story. I have educated you on the fun involving two normal bodily functions. All of us kids constantly looked for any way to enjoy God's creation. In Dubuque, Iowa every Friday night, junior high kids went to Teen-Town at the YWCA for a dance. We met kids from the other junior high school and danced or stood around and talked. No boys danced to the fast dances. We only did the slow ones and watched the girls dance with each other during the fast ones.

We walked the four miles to the "Y." We walked everywhere then. Most of our parents were already into a euchre game at one of the numerous neighborhood bars when it was time for us to leave. They would not have taken us anyway or picked us up either. As we left at the pre-determined time, I remembered smelling the typical Friday evening dinner from open windows in the North End. Sauerkraut, pork roast, and potato salad were the fare of all German families. The aroma hung on to the sidewalks as more kids joined in the trek to Teen Town. Many families went out to dinner for all-you-can-eat-catfish on Friday evenings. This tradition is practiced yet today by Dubuquers.

Traditions like those are nice. You know what is coming and what to expect. The five of us guys met up every Friday night for the dance. It was our tradition. Rex joined me as we headed down Lincoln Avenue and met Tom at the corner of Kniest Street. Jim then showed up about fifteen minutes later at Five Points. This was an intersection so named because five different streets met at one intersection. Jim was always late. He told us that sauerkraut gave him gas and he wanted to practice his skill in his bedroom.

He also spilled the beans (no pun intended), when he told us how he and Rex were recording their singing along with music from a forty-five rpm record. Rex halted the recording of a George Jones song, *"The Race Is On."* He took the mic, held it next to his butt cheeks and farted at the exact point of *"And the winner loses all."* We were proud of them both.

We turned left on to Elm Street and met Kosta who was sitting on the curb smoking and waiting for us. We never did cross the tracks and enter the Flats at night to look for him. It was not safe so he came out to meet up with us.

Some thirty minutes later there we were standing around watching the girls dance. Some kids just stood there with their right hands in their pockets. Every now and then there was a mad scramble in all directions when Jim cut one loose. One time he came up to me and whispered, "Sauerkraut."

The dance always ended with a slow song and I would dart in and out of bodies looking for my girlfriend and hoped they would play our song. It was *Blue Velvet* by Bobby Vinton. It was a great cheek-to-cheek dance. Promptly at ten o'clock the lights came on and the place closed. Now it was time for action.

After drinking at least six cups of pop, our bladders were about to explode. We each kept this under control hoping we might win the first place blue ribbon at the Great Piddling Contest. It was a tradition to compete against one another to see who could pee the furthest into the street while standing and balancing on the curb.

Four of us tried diligently to beat Kosta but we never could. He was the champion piddler.

As he walked along the street, it was beautiful to see his work on every corner and his work on every tree. Us kids watched on with amazement, as Kosta was all the rage. It impressed us that a kid from the Flats was the piddler of the age. We all lined up behind him with instinct true to start a piddlin' contest to see Kosta through. So on we went peeing by scraps, and piles, and ruts until the last of us was a piddlin' only dust. Then Kosta gave an expedition on different ways to piddle. Here a burst, there a squirt, sometimes just a dribble. He had more pretend blue ribbons than I could ever win running sprints during Track & Field.

There were times when my girlfriend stayed in town at her aunt's home. She lived out in the country and most times her parents picked her up after Teen-Town. On those occasions where she stayed in town, I was able to walk her to the aunt's house the three miles away. It took quite some time as we stopped to kiss about every one-hundred yards.

"Dave, what are you doing? Stop that," she demanded as I pushed my body up against hers.

We were standing against the metal fence that surrounded Fulton Elementary School. I should say she was standing with her back against the fence and I was next to her. There was no daylight between us. I was like a dog in heat.

"The last time you did this I had the fence pattern on my back for the whole week-end." she complained.

I gave the issue a rest and obliged her command. I laughed, "Yeah, I remember you telling me that. I like to call it my "waffle move." Maybe I could use it wrestling."

She gave me a gentle slap on my left shoulder and we kissed again.

There is one final part to the Peeing Contest I would like to share. It was at one of our reunions many years later and the old gang was reminiscing. We were standing around watching the women dance. I noticed there were no hands in the pockets. I asked Kosta about the peeing contest and how the heck he beat us. He leaned into our circle and replied, "I had diabetes."

We all called him a bastard.

Research is currently being done with cow manure to determine if it can somehow be used for energy.

David Nelson Nelson

"Bobo: The Lucky Strike Chimp"

"Hey, Jim, do you think there will be any good looking Catholic girls up at Skate Town tonight?" Tom asked as the four of us walked past Spahn and Rose Lumber Yard and made the turn on Rhomberg Avenue toward the final northern border of Dubuque.

Skate Town was a place where teens and even little kids went on weekends. Across the gravel parking lot was the Point Go Cart Track & Miniature Golf. At the back end of the lot in a darkened corner beneath the 300-foot drop from the Eagle Point Park look-off was a dilapidated zoo. Well, not really a zoo, but more of a prison for a few animals. It consisted of four cages that housed a lion, a peacock, and two rhesus macaques – chimps, as we knew them. Kids of all ages were scattered about either eating cotton candy, waiting their turns in line for the next available go-cart or yelling because they missed shooting their final golf ball into the clown's mouth for a free game of miniature golf. Across the street was the western bank of the Mississippi River and one block away was the bridge that connected Iowa to Wisconsin. It literally was the end of our stomping ground.

Jim laughed out loud, "Why do you care about Catholic girls, Tom? You're a non-Catholic and they want nothing to do with you. Sides, they don't put out anyway. All the nuns have 'em brainwashed into joining the convent when they get older."

Just as we turned into the gravel parking lot, Captain Masters sped past us in his car after dropping off one or more of his children. He was a World War II veteran who also was an alcoholic and never attended Sacred Heart Church like his wife and seven kids did. Every Sunday he had his own ritual of sitting on his front porch swing drinking coffee spiked with vodka, reading the *Telegraph Herald* and watching the flock migrate northward into church. It was always fun to watch him when the bells from the church rang out. If they caught him off guard he would hit the ground, cover his head and lie in a curled position. Captain Marshall as he insisted we call him, did odd jobs fixing cars for others in the area. Then he went straight to the bar across the street from his house to drink away the money he earned. All the kids in his family were left to roam the streets as they pleased.

Kosta told me that there were drunks at the Airport Inn who had similar reactions to the Captain. He said older kids would light firecrackers and throw them under the bar stools to watch many of the WW II veterans hit the floor cowering in fear.

Jim lectured, "Now I don't know if Catholic girls put out any more or less than the non-Catholic ones. I do know they let ya into their bras easier because that is only a minor sin. Now a major sin would be if you made it into their panties. That would be a big deal and a big sin. The non-Catholic girls don't know about all these sin levels, so me, I figure they are fair game."

"I want to see the Bobo do his thing and I have a fresh pack of Lucky Strikes to get him going," I said. "This will be fun."

"Nelson, you are one sick nimrod," Tom laughed. Seeing the lights ahead and hearing Bobby Vinton sing over the loud speakers, we picked up the pace.

"Aw, leave him alone. That's what neat about this. There's something for each of us," Kosta said as he shoved Rich while Rex grabbed my right arm.

"Holy Cow. Look at the knockers on that one in the tight pink shorts," Rex said pointing to an older girl skating backwards. "Hey you guys, I'm going to hang out here for a while."

We walked past a few parked cars to the sounds of a couple hundred children from ages six to eighteen. They were skating, playing miniature golf, riding in go-karts, or just hanging around. Many of the older boys leaned against their cars bragging about one thing or another.

The teenage boys wore the dress of the day for 1963. Blue jeans with the lower pant leg rolled up once, white T-shirt with both sleeves rolled up to expose the muscled arms and black boots of any style they chose. The left arm sleeve was used to carry a package of cigarettes between the skin and the white cotton fabric. The hairstyle was either a butch or a flattop. Longer hair was worn with a D-A (duck's ass) in the back. That was where hair from the right and left sides of the head met in the middle and held in place with either Vitalis or Brylcream hair gels. They drove 1950s cars and always sat on the car hoods checking out the girls.

Tom stopped dead in his tracks to lean against the rail of the skating rink a few feet from Rex. They listened to another slow song and watched the older girls skate. Jim went to the line to ride a go-cart and Kosta went to get a pop at the concession stand. Me, I headed right for Bobo's cage in the back of the complex. The cage area did not have direct lights but only the faint edges from the main lighting reserved for people by the go-kart track. After all, these were just animals and did not require special treatment.

I didn't say a word as I walked toward the cage and saw some eight year olds throwing gravel at a lion. The worn out, shell of a beast just stood there, turned, and changed directions from the tiny pellets being flung at it.

In the cage next to the lion was, Bobo, the chimp. He was hanging his paws out through the chicken wire fence watching everyone as we watched him. Every few seconds he would pucker his lips, scratch his butt and then lick his fingers. I always liked it when he scratched his head as if to gather some distant thought and then picked a bug from his hide and ate it. If anyone came too close, Bobo had the ability to quickly stretch his arm through the fence and try to touch him or maybe even snatch a ball cap from an unsuspecting kid.

"Hey, you kids, do you want to see something funny," I yelled to the eight year old boys who appeared frustrated by the lack of response from the lion in the next cage over.

"Sure," one of them said as the five came running toward Bobo's cage.

"OK watch this." I tapped the full pack of Luckies from the bottom to release the first cigarette.

"Oh, Bobo, Bobo look what I have," I called out as I held my hand entirely flat with a lit cigarette balanced off the side of my palm.

Bobo went berserk screaming, pulling at the fence and shaking it, jumping down and back up! Then he ran across the few limbs inside the cage spilling his water dish. The kids all screamed in unison and one fell to the gravel trying to run away. Moments later they returned and this time they were more cautious.

"Hey, mister why did he go nuts from that," one kid asked.

"Because he likes to smoke and if you watch real close you will see what else he can do," I enticed them as they gathered around me.

"All right, watch this," I said as I took a deep drag off the cigarette and again placed it on to my open palm with the lit end hanging off the side.

Bobo settled down this time and had his right arm stretched through the wire fence and held his body to it with both legs and his left arm. He lifted the cigarette with precision like a surgeon reaching for a scalpel and placed the end into his mouth. The kids laughed and shoved one another and could not believe their eyes.

"Keep watching. You haven't seen anything yet."

They quieted to a hush and then it happened. The pink end of his pecker emerged and an erection developed. There he was puffing and hanging on the fence with an erection sticking out for all to see. Now the kids really howled. I heard phrases like "Holy Crap," "Oh my God," and "Do youse see that." I was so pleased with myself because I'd brought joy into the lives of others if only for a brief minute.

Then Bobo did something to leave a mark in the memory of all who now gathered about the cage. He started masturbating! Yep, flogging his dong, whacking his puppy, beatin' his meat. The whole time he just kept puffing and blowing smoke without ever removing the cigarette from his lips. Still holding on to the side of the cage with his left arm and legs he shook the entire fence while whacking off.

The boys were hysterical, little girls ran away, and the lion roared at the commotion. The sound of crunching gravel from people running got louder. The older boys came running from their parked cars, kids ran from the go-kart section, and teen-aged girls stopped skating and leaned over the rails to see what was happening.

Rex sprinted past the teen-aged boys, Tom dropped his putter and charged to the darkened lot, and Jim ran from the go-cart line. Cool Kosta walked.

"Oh sure, Nelson. I figured it was you over here either telling jokes or doing something to create some chaos," Jim laughed.

Rex shoved some little kids out of the way so he could get a better view. Tom went around the far left side so he could see. Kosta parted the crowd with his presence and walked toward the cage. He took one look, turned toward me, and said, "Nelson, you are one sick puppy."

And that was the highlight of my night. I wondered if it was a major or minor sin for the Catholics to see a masturbating chimp. Me, I could care less. I was a non-Catholic. I figured Bobo didn't know Marilyn Monroe was dead.

A few nights later I received another lecture from Veronica about my behavior with Bobo. She told me I was a pervert. I just smiled on the other end of the phone. When asked how she heard about it, she said Rex told her during band practice.

"Ah, that bastard," I thought.

PALS: Part One

"Changing the Way America Does Business"

As a juvenile delinquent I never harmed a person physically – except for Danny on the trampoline in gym class. I had enough physical abuse from my dad and knew from experience it was wrong to hurt those less fortunate or weaker than myself. That was my unwritten code. I suppose that is why, as an adult, I have helped the less fortunate and deprived individuals in our society.

A childhood memory I have is going to bed hungry quite often. The thick, heavy, summer evening air penetrated my open bedroom window. I fell asleep each night soaking wet from sweat. The stink from the Dubuque Packing House permeated my room. It also permeated my entire house. In the winters I was unable to get warm in bed during thirty-day stretches of below zero Iowa winters. It was not unusual for us to dress next to the open oven-door in the kitchen.

And yet, there were many other children who had it worse. One time I saw a kid in the cafeteria open his faded, metal Roy Rogers lunch box. He had four crackers and a thermos of milk that must have been warm from being in his locker all morning. I bought ice cream for dessert with money I stole from my older sister's purse. I felt awful seeing that kid slowly eat his first cracker. I closed the lid on my ice cream and slid it across the table to him and simply said, "Here." He nodded a thanks to me.

While people were off limits, their property never was. If anyone had something I did not, then they were fair game. From the time I stole that pear all Hell broke loose in my life. In elementary school four of us stole a two-by-twelve-inch board eight feet long from the Span and Rose Lumber Company. It was located at the far North End near Municipal Swimming Pool and Skate-Town. We walked that plank right out the door, carried it about a mile to where Dubuque ends and the railroad tracks continued. We walked the tracks to Flat Rock and stuck it into a huge rock that jutted out into the backwaters of the Mississippi next to the lock and dam. It was our private diving board for the day. Pretty cool, I'd say.

One time, I didn't want to walk the mile or so to the house from the swimming pool. I took my pick of the best bicycle propped up near the front door. As big as you please, I hopped on after securing my wet trunks and towel to the rack over the back bumper. I never gave a concern and slowly peddled towards Rhomberg Avenue. Four blocks from the pool, I turned by Holy Trinity Church and thought of Jim. Three blocks from my house on Lincoln was Bethany Nursing Home. The porch was lined with elderly devoted Lutherans who were living out their last days. I came to a screech with pressure on the back brakes and shoved the bike between two parked cars. After removing my towel and trunks I began walking towards my house.

"Hey, Sonny youse forgot your bicycle. It's right there by the curb. Hey, Sonny," an old lady in a wheelchair yelled over the brick-lined porch.

Stealing bicycles on a regular basis probably led to the development of a cottage industry in America. It was the creation of the chain and lock system to prevent theft.

I continued with my business of walking home wondering if I would once again be the target of my dad's rage or if I would be denied supper for being late. If any of us kids were late for supper we were not allowed to eat and had to do all the dishes. I made it home in the nick of time as everyone was heading toward the kitchen when I entered the front door.

I regularly stole pop bottles from behind local grocery stores and took them into the front doors selling them back to the owners. I was not greedy. I stole enough to gain the ten- cents entry into Municipal Pool. At two cents a bottle that was pretty easy. Eventually progress came along and aluminum cans were more popular than the bottles.

I stole stick-matches from the Catholic Churches. Near the altar, there were candles that could be lit and a prayer said for someone. Next to the rows of red candles I found stacks of stick matches. I used the matches to light my cigarettes that I stole from my mother or when things were just right I managed to steal an entire carton from Eagles Grocery Store. When times were slim I would walk the gutters looking for cigarette butts that adults or teenagers had thrown out the windows of their cars. One time I was caught red-handed by a priest at Holy Trinity. He asked me what I was doing and what parish did I attend. I told him Sacred Heart. That was a lie. I was a non-Catholic who had infiltrated the enemy lines.

"Hey, I have to go to Eagles Grocery Store for my ma. Do you want to see if we can steal a carton of smokes like Hank and I did a couple years ago," I asked Tom.

Pushing his black framed glasses back to their resting place on the bridge of his nose he said," Sure. I swear, Nelson you are going to get me carded at the police station like you have what two or three times already?"

"Oh, it's no big deal. All they do is write a bunch of stuff on a recipe card, call your folks and let you go. The first time was pretty scary but after that it was a walk in the park," I bragged.

"I know you already told me how you and Hank stole the cigarettes last time but tell me again so it's clear in my head and we don't get caught," he demanded.

"OK. We get a cart and buy all the groceries first. One of the things we put into the cart is a carton of cigarettes and we just keep shopping. Ya know where they have that pop machine in the back corner of the store next to the water cooler," I asked as he nodded. "We'll push the cart full of groceries next to the cooler and while you get a drink, I'll take the carton of cigarettes and hide them between the pop machine and the water cooler.

We then go and check out, and as I pay for the stuff you say that you want a pop and do it kind of loud. The workers will then know what we are doing carrying our couple bags of groceries back into the food area. While you take your time looking for change and thereby blocking my view, I will set the bags down on the floor next to the cooler. You get your pop while I bend down to tie my shoe. When you give the "all clear" sign I will reach by the cooler and put the carton into the bag. Whatever you do don't panic. It's just like the time we stole that plank for our diving board at flat rock. Act like you own the place. If we should get caught, blame it on the checker and we say she must have forgotten to enter it on the bill."

"Oh crap. This is kind of frightening but also exciting. I swear you always think everything through so well," he laughed with a he-he-he.

"That kind of thinking is needed to survive at home. If I ever get caught I will leave more of my skin on the basement floor from the old man's whippings."

Everything went as planned and a block from the store, Tom slapped my left shoulder and with a grin said, "Way to go! You were right that was nothing. Where do you want to have a smoke?"

"Up there," I said pointing to two billboards a block away at Five Points. "We can climb the poles using the metal bars like the workers do and squeeze behind the signs. There's a plank to stand on behind that sign closer to us. It'll be a little tight but nobody will ever notice us even with all that traffic."

The workers at the gas station next to the billboards didn't notice the two grocery bags on the ground. The passing motorists driving Garfield Avenue, Rhomberg Avenue and Elm Street paid no attention to two little kids climbing behind the signs for an afternoon smoke on a hot July day in the North End of Dubuque.

"Jeez, it's tight in here. It's kind of hard to even light up. Even so it's fun," Tom complained. "Did you steal those stick matches from Sacred Heart?"

Coughing a couple times I just shook my head yes and blew smoke into the air that wrapped around the front of the billboards. Stolen cigarettes always tasted the best. I would like to think my little foolproof method of stealing cigarettes changed the way America's grocery stores did business. Cigarettes are now locked in glass cases or behind the counter.

I am not certain why, but in junior high school I stole gas caps from parked cars. Some people collected stamps. Some collected coins. I collected stolen gas caps. I had a sundry collection from every make and model throughout my neighborhood. I do not know to this day why I did that. But do any of us know why we did certain things then or now?

In the 1950s and 60s, cars did not have locked gas cap covers. It was a walk in the park - so to speak. I would walk by a car, open the lid covering the cap, and with a quick turn to the left I released the cap and put it into my paper sack like a kid collecting candy at Halloween. This occurred for over a year. I took them home and climbed into the loft of our ram-shackled garage and put them into an old metal diaper pail. When that was full I started loading them into a storage trunk. I guess I did it just because I could.

Years later the auto industry developed lockable gas covers that could only be released from inside the car. I like to think I had an influence on America's auto industry like I did with the pop machines, cigarettes, and bicycles.

By the way, thousands of years ago, Egyptians used a tall stone pillar to publicize laws and treaties. This unique form of communication was the early form of outdoor advertising and the predecessor of modern billboards.

David Nelson Nelson

"The Dubuque Packers"

The Dubuque Star Brewery is on The United States National Register of Historic Places. The Romanesque architectural style has never changed since it was constructed in 1899. Across the street from the brewery once stood a minor league baseball complex from 1915 through 1976. Today, there is a casino, hotel and parking lot. The baseball team was known as The Dubuque Packers. The field hosted the Packers from 1954 through 1976. The Packers was a farm team for the Chicago White Sox, Pittsburg Pirates, Cleveland Indians, Los Angeles Dodgers, and the Houston Astros. Some notable players from Dubuque included: Tommy John, Steve Yeager, Tommy Agee, Joe Rudi, and Terry Puhl. Kids between the ages of eight and thirteen could have cared less back in the late 50s and early 60s about the players. It was simply a place for us to go and play. We rarely watched the games.

Many children wanted to became a member of the Knot Hole Club. The organization was free to join and each night we were given one free bottle of pop and one hot dog. We had our own set of bleachers on the far third base side. Our only responsibility was to shag balls that went over the fence. We were required to return them and in exchange, we all were allowed into the game free of charge.

There was no parented oversight. Tom and I walked the four miles using the sidewalk on Elm Street. Once we passed the Flats and it was safe to do so, we cut up onto the railroad tracks and followed them to Petrakis Baseball Park. The process was reversed for our late night return home.

Outside the tin walls of the field was a lumberyard where stacks of timber were piled as high as the stars. At least that is what it seemed like to me. We would scale the various sized mountains of stacked boards. We would flip boards among the stacks to create bridges that allowed us to run from one pile to another. Some bridges went uphill while others went down. Some crossings were straight. Others had a sharp turn halfway across. When we fell off,

PALS: Part One

that was our clue to pretend to be dead and we had to lie in the dirt for thirty-seconds before re-joining the game of tag. Each time I scaled a pile, I felt like King Kong climbing that building in New York - Powerful and Untouchable.

Our game was interrupted by an occasional foul ball or home run rising from the Packer's game inside the fence. The rule was that all the Knot Hole Members had to charge around the outside walls of the ballpark seeking the prize. It was like a treasure hunt on the run. Sometimes there were thirty dirty-faced kids, wet with sweat screaming and running after a single ball.

Even now when I think about those times and close my eyes I can still hear the distinct crack of a ball contacting a Louisville Slugger. One night long ago, I heard the crowd roar with excitement and looked over to see the fog covering the poorly lit field. I saw the ball float high over the cloud of fog in center field and disappear. The heck with me playing dead, I thought. I could have a head start for the trophy.

Kids jumped from low piles, scampered across bridges heading for firmer ground, and one kid even jumped from the highest of all mountains. He may not have been pretending to play dead from the long fall.

Because of my speed and the head start, I was in the lead. I was going to be the first one there, I thought. I made the turn around left field from third base. My arms were stretching out in front of me, my little legs were pumping, and I thought of the phrase, "faster than a speeding bullet" heard every Saturday watching Superman. I was focused on my job. There were no footsteps near me. I heard kids laughing back by left field as I was nearing center field.

I made the final turn and there it was, my prize ball plopped in the dirt in the well- lit area behind the park's wall. The leather-covered, white stitched ball was waiting for me to reach out and grab it. I took one look and decided against going any further. I made an immediate 180-degree turn, shifted into fifth gear, and raced like Jesse Owens. As I passed several kids going the other way, they looked confused and noticed I had no ball in my hand.

What I did have was a vivid memory of a two-foot long river rat sitting on its hind legs next to the ball. I saw the whites of his teeth, long pointed claws, and twisted eyebrows. I kept running for another three blocks and finally quit to catch my breath. I never returned to shag balls. That homerun made me quit the Knot Hole Club.

Walking into civics class at Jeff the first time gave me a flashback. Popeye Barnum reminded me of that rat.

PALS: Part One

"Popeye"

"Just so I know, and I don't even have to ask, but are you going to do what we all talked about in Popeye's class tomorrow," Veronica asked over the phone.

"Well now what do you think? I heard Rex was not in on it because he's afraid," I told her.

Veronica giggled. "Of what? What a chicken! Jeez, he needs to get with it."

I smiled in satisfaction. "He's afraid if we get caught he'll not be our class president anymore."

She took a long breath into the phone. "Uh, if the whole class does it, nothing is going to happen. You and Kosta need to put the fear into him."

Popeye was our current events teacher in the ninth grade. We were in her class once a week and that was way too much because it was beyond boring. Kosta said it was his favorite class because she showed filmstrips almost weekly and he slept quite well in the darkened room.

One time, however, Kosta was startled when the lights came on because Popeye had to fix the filmstrip. He sat up straight and was disoriented for a moment. Those kids around him laughed because he had lines on his face from the pressure of his head resting on his arms. Earlier that day Rex had snuck into the room while it was empty. He took a marker and wrote on a seven-foot length of the movie. Popeye had to reel the filmstrip by hand until there was a clean area. We all thought it was pretty funny but Kosta called Rex a bastard because the prank caused him to lose some great sleep.

Popeye had terrible vision and wore thick glasses that rested on the lower part of her nose. Had she worn them correctly she might have seen the time Jim stuck an entire box of raisins on the windows. She removed a fly swatter from her desk drawer and proceeded to hit them one by one while speaking to us about some worthless topic.

If Popeye had her glasses up just a little further on her nose, she might have caught me when I crawled up the aisle during a filmstrip and snatched the shoe off Veronica's foot. Gliding down the aisle using the duck-walk I learned in gym class, I made it to the window undetected. I threw her shoe out the window to the grassy field below. Veronica and I did not talk on the phone that night. Rex, Jim, Tom and I all laughed about it. Kosta was sleeping and missed the action.

Popeye's black, wiry and short hair was cropped close to her large head. The flowered dresses she wore fell off her skinny frame. Her most prominent feature was her eyebrows. They were long, large and out of control. They went in every direction and projected over her scooped out and sunken face. Had she not worn a dress she might have been mistaken for a little old man. As a matter of fact she reminded all of us of the popular comedian at the time, Groucho Marx. How she came to be named Popeye was anybody's guess. We learned it from the older kids. They probably learned it from the really older kids.

And so it was we were about to pull the coup de grace of all school kid pranks. During one of her filmstrips, and at the right moment, all of us dropped a book on the floor. We were a little late initially because someone had to wake Kosta. With Popeye sitting at her desk at the front of the room, we did it. We all acted in unison. Smack. Twenty-five books hit the floor in stereo. Rex was in on it also.

Popeye jumped up, ran to the door, turned the lights on and to our absolute amazement began clapping her hands together. "Okay, students quickly now we have a fire drill."

The entire class was still in a manic state of laughter by the time we reached the end of the hall, with Popeye in the lead. Some kids were wiping their eyes, others held their ribs, and I saw a group of three girls hanging off one another laughing hysterically. When we made it the end of the hall, Popeye calmly said, "Well, I guess it was a false alarm."

Twenty-five different styles of laughter erupted on the second floor of Jefferson Junior High that day.

By contrast, it was in Popeye's room on November 22nd of that year when Coach came in and told us President Kennedy was dead. There was no laughter that day.

"I never forget a face, but in this case I'll be glad to make an exception."
                                        -Groucho Marx

David Nelson Nelson

"You Should Stick to Track"

"Hey, are you going to try out for the operetta?" Veronica asked during one of our evening phone calls.

"I don't know. I guess I'll have to being as I am in the Glee Club. It sounds kind of stupid to me though."

"Everyone is going to be in it. Well, not Kosta, but all the rest of us."

"Oh yeah, speaking of Kosta, he gave you a compliment today walking home from school."

"What! Kosta? Jeez, he never compliments anyone." She giggled. "What did he say?"

"He said how much he appreciated you never judging him because of where he lives. You know, he never wants anybody to see his house. We're best friends and I don't even know which house is his in the Flats."

"That was nice of him, but that's just me. That's how I am to all of you guys."

"That reminds me, Veronica. I thought of this before but never asked you. Why do you seem to have mostly guy friends? You're like one of us and that is pretty neat and all, but I was just wondering."

"It's only 'cuz you and I are best friends, Dave that I'll tell you. I've always found it easier to be friends with boys rather than girls. I don't know why. It's just that way. Some of the other girls don't accept me because of that."

"Ah, I don't think that's true. Everyone likes you."

"No, I'm being serious. That was very nice what Kosta said about me. So getting back to my question, are you trying out or not?"

"What the heck is a Pinafore? I never heard of such a thing."

"Dave, it's a ship. If you'd pay attention in Popeye's class you'd have learned that. It was when we talked about the tall ships."

Two weeks later I was memorizing the words that I had to sing and speak in the ninth grade production of The H.M.S. Pinafore. Veronica played the part of Josephine. Rex was Captain Corcoran (father of Josephine). Sir Joseph Porter was played by Frank, Connie played Little Buttercup, I was Bill Bobstay, and Larry was Dick Deadeye.

The production included probably half of our class. Students were playing many roles, from sailors to cousins to aunts. Tom and several other students helped create the set and the public donated costumes, supplies, and labor.

The performance was indeed quite fun and went off without a hitch. We entertained the PTA and general public in our school auditorium on June 4th and 5th, 1964 at 8 P.M. To this day, many of us still know our lines and songs.

I was a soprano in the Boy's Glee Club. In the ninth grade all my friends' voices were changing. I still sounded like a girl when I sang. In the group there was Frank, Dave, Bob, Jim, Dennis, Rex, me and several others. We performed at functions around Dubuque singing songs such as "The Whiffenpoof Song" and "I Want A Girl."

The singing group was led my Mrs. Ava Giles. She was always nice to me, in a strict sort of way. I once did my rendition of some dirty songs when she left the room. I completed my last note, the guys started screaming with laughter, and in she walked clamping her jaws. There was total silence. Stopping a good laugh is as bad as stopping a fart mid-way through, or ending a pee when there's still more to come. None of them are much fun.

"Would you like to share with me, Dave what you shared with the others?"

"No, thanks," I said as I lowered my gaze to the floor.

Mrs. Giles tapped her pencil on the piano top. "Uh huh, I didn't think so."

A few months later we were practicing songs for the monthly PTA Meeting to be held in the auditorium. It was because of the success of the operetta that we were asked to entertain. I had the highest of all voices and was the shortest of all boys.

We gathered backstage behind the curtains. We were to walk out, single file with me being the last in line. We sang our three songs for the PTA and I did as instructed. I was to lead the entire group off stage and the plan was we were to continue singing up the aisle and out the door to the hallway.

That night was one of the most embarrassing moments of my life. The others in the group went back stage, through the fire door, down the fire escape, and were outside laughing as they pulled the prank on me. I didn't realize this until about halfway up the aisle, I heard only myself screeching for the crowd. It was the longest walk of my life. There in the hallway door stood Coach with his arms folded leaning against the doorjamb.

"You should stick to running track," he said quietly

The next day Kosta shot pop out his nostrils and almost choked when I told him the story. "Nelson, you're such a chump."

PALS: Part One

"I'm the Captain of the sea.
And when I've married thee,
I'll be true to your sisters, and your cousins and your aunts
Especially your cousins who are numbered by the dozens..."

David Nelson Nelson

"Jesse Owens"

There were many constants in my life during those years. I look back and smile to myself about the laughter with friends, lighting farts, eating pizza every Sunday evening at Tom's house, talking with Veronica on the phone, and being the best athlete I could be for the Jefferson J-Hawks.

I don't look back and smile at all the constants in my life then; the days of being beaten, or kicked, forced to stand at attention in a corner of a room, and other abuse from my dad. All those events, both positive and negative made me what I am today. I now embrace all of them. The one constant in my life that eventually took me out of the North End as I planned was track & field and the excellence I was able to achieve.

I noticed at around age eight I had a gift for running, not just regular running, but fast. I even promised myself that one day I would be the fastest runner in Dubuque and use that skill to someday get away and start a new life. I worked hard and set a couple records in individual events at Jeff. Rex was also quite fast. He and I along with Tom Schweikert and another kid named Tom set some relay records.

I also was on the wrestling team. As a matter of fact, when I was in the ninth grade I wrestled for the high school across town. There was another ninth grader from the other junior high school who also wrestled for the high school. A coach would come to Jeff and pick me up but I had to walk home after practice. Dubuque Senior High School needed a ninety pounder and did not have one. So, I wrestled in that slot and earned my school letter before attending the tenth grade.

In the summer after the ninth grade, there was a track meet that was called "The Junior Olympics." There were try-outs for kids of all ages in every type of event. I was the fastest in my age group for the 100- yard dash and was going to run at the Des Moines' Drake Stadium against other kids my age. Rex was there and he too was in the 100-yard dash and the long jump. There were many kids from Jeff who qualified.

"Hey, did you hear?" I asked Veronica.

"Hear what?" She giggled. "What kind of trouble are you in now? I don't know about you, Nelson. Jeez, I don't know if I am ready for this one."

"I've been chosen to ride in a parade in Dubuque with none other than my hero, Jesse Owens!"

She screamed so loud I held the phone away from my ear. "Oh, my God! Dave I am so proud of you. We have to get the gang together and go downtown and watch you. Jeez, Nelson you go from one extreme to another."

The Dubuque Recreation Department planned a parade for all of us kids representing Dubuque. I was asked to ride in a convertible with none other than my idol at the time, Jesse Owens. In the 1936 Olympics held in Berlin, Germany and in front of Adolf Hitler, Owens won gold medals in the 100- and 200- yard dashes, the long jump, and was on America's 4x100 relay. Yes, that Jesse Owens. He was a student at Ohio State University when he was in the Olympics.

Years earlier I'd read about his personal life. His dad was a sharecropper and his grandparents had been slaves. I used to think I was Jesse when I ran. In fact, I once dreamed he and I were on the same relay team. There I was sitting in a Cadillac convertible next to my hero during a parade in downtown Dubuque. It was awesome. We had just left Washington Park when off to my right I heard, "Hey, Nelson, Nelson. Over here."

I looked to see the five smiling faces of my pals. Veronica was jumping up and down while Tom was adjusting his glasses with one hand and waving with another. Rex gave a thumbs up and a big smile, while Jim gave me the finger as he pretended to scratch his nose. Kosta was cool when he uncrossed his arms and waved his right hand from waist level.

The streets were lined three deep and I sucked in the cheering as if I just won the 100-Yard Dash. I could not keep from smiling as I waved to the crowd on both sides of the street. I noticed how Jesse was such an easy person to speak with. He showed respect for this stranger, this punk ninth grader.

"Dave, I want to leave you with this piece of advice," he said when the parade ended and the car turned down a side street.

I figured he would give me hints about the starting block position, leaning forward at the start, or something about my finish. But no, what he said has never left me. "The most important thing in life," he said, "is to remember somebody's name. You'll go a long way with that tip."

I looked him right into his left eye and gave an understanding nod. And then something happened that bonded us together even further. He asked the driver to stop so he could buy a package of cigarettes. Jesse Owens was a smoker too.

A month later I was at a dinner for the participants of the Junior Olympics. There at the front table was Jesse Owens. I walked up to him, stuck out my hand and said, "Hi, Jesse."

"Why, hello, Dave," he said as he shook my hand several times.

He remembered my name. Jesse Owens remembered my name.

The year was 1935. It was to be the accomplishment of a lifetime. In 45 minutes on a spring afternoon he established three world records and tied another. He ran the 100-yard dash in 9.4 seconds to tie the world record. In his only long jump attempt, he leaped 26feet, 8 and ¼ inches. That world record stood for twenty-

five years. His 20.3 seconds in the 220-yard dash became another world record. He was the first person in the world to break 23 seconds in the 220-yard low hurdles with a time of 22.6 seconds.

David Nelson Nelson

"He Winds Up. Here's the Pitch"

The area by the Municipal pool had quite a bit to offer kids of all ages. There was the Point Drive-In with carhops on roller skates. They had nice legs and wore short shorts for everyone to admire. Ice cream cones were five cents each. The bowling alley offered entertainment for everyone and was open from noon until midnight. The main channel of the Mississippi River was a mere one hundred fifty yards away from the bowling alley. Barges, tug boats, paddle wheel boats and small watercraft pulling people on skis were all a regular occurrence for watching land lovers. At the end of the bowling alley parking lot was the 16th Street channel that created a peninsula with the main river channel on the other side. On the backside of the bowling alley were three baseball fields.

Despite so much to do and so much to see, we were delinquents back then, pure and simple. Take the time that Jim and I discovered a trashcan full of empty pop bottles next to the dugout in one of those ball fields I just mentioned.

"So, Jimmy boy, you think you're a good pitcher, do you," I asked as I grabbed a handful of bottles and headed out towards the mound.

He knew exactly what was up with my challenge and joined me in carrying an arm full of bottles. "OK, whoever smashes a bottle against that steel pipe behind home plate gets a home run. If the bottle breaks, but not from the pipe, we get a triple. If it does not break, the inning is over and the next guy is up."

Smack, pop, crash was heard that afternoon as we competed to be number one. It was so exciting we could barely contain ourselves as we ran back and forth to the garbage can gathering more bottles to throw. We laughed and teased one another and at times even shoved the other off the mound when the wind-up took place. This was much better than watching bowlers, boats in the river and boobs at the pool. Warren Spahn with the Milwaukee

Braves was no better than us. Mickey Mantle or Roger Maris could not have hit our pitches. We were impressed with ourselves - until Officer Degnan drove up.

"Oh crap," Jim said. "Some jerk must have called the cops. Jeez, kids can't even have fun."

Officer Degnan stood next to the open door of his squad car. Just the sight of him ticked me off. He motioned with his flexing index finger for us to come to him.

"What," I asked innocently.

I turned to look at center field as if there were other kids around who had created this mess. "Now. Youse get over to me this very minute. Don't make me come into the field and get youse two punks."

It was one of those things where you have no choice. Jim snickered as we approached the squad car. "We may be punks but at least we're not fat like him," I whispered.

"Something funny with you, kid," he said looking at Jim.

Jim swallowed hard. "No."

"Now what the Sam Hell were youse guys doing making all this mess? Get in the back seat and I need some information from the two of youse."

After writing down our names, addresses and phone numbers, he said he was taking us to the station on Central Avenue to be carded.

Oh crap. I thought about another beating from my dad. One way or another I was in deep trouble being taken in by the cops again.

Officer Degnan glared at me in the rear view mirror of the squad car. "I know you," he said, "Your name is Nelson, isn't it?" I nodded but did not speak.

"I won." Jim said. "I beat your rear end. You stink at being a pitcher. You need to play right field where they put all the losers."

"You did not win. The score was tied and I lost my turn to pitch when Barney Fife drove up," I said as Jim giggled. "And besides right field is where Mickey plays and he's no loser."

Officer Degnan's eyes glared at me in the mirror. "What did you say about me being Barney Fife?"

"Nothing." I said as we turned onto 16th Street.

"You're a real punk, a hoodlum. That too will go in my report."

Biting the inside of my cheek, I watched kids playing baseball out the window of the squad car in a dirt lot and wondered if Mean Boy was among them. One kid shot a bird toward the car from a long way off. Yep, that has to be Mean Boy, I thought.

"What happens now?" Jim asked me when we were told to sit on the hard wooden bench in the hallway at the police station.

"Probably nothing to you. They'll write some stuff on their recipe cards, call your folks and have them come pick you up. Me, I'll get pulverized by my old man."

What felt like hours later, Officer Degnan returned to us sitting on the hard bench in the hallway of the police station. "It's been one hour since we called both of your houses and the Captain said for me to let both of youse go. But that's ok. We'll call your houses again tonight or tomorrow. Youse are free to go."

PALS: Part One

Feeling cocky, I couldn't help myself, "Can we get a ride back up to the ball field? It's a long walk and after all you are the one who drove us down here."

Officer Degnan didn't say a word. He didn't have to as his eyes spoke volumes. His frown created one long eyebrow as he peered through the slits in his eyes, the veins on his neck pulsed and his facial color turned bright red. He stood at attention and pointed to the front door.

"I guess that means no," I said to a laughing-out-loud Jim.

"Can we get a ride? Can we get a ride?" Jim teased in a high imitating pitch. "I can't believe you said that. You're one crazy maniac, Nelson. Do you want to come home and spend the night at my house and have supper with us?"

Anything to delay a guaranteed beating would be nice and so I said, "Great. Thanks."

An hour later, we left Lincoln Avenue and walked up Shiras Blvd. A kid about our age was bending down at the curb picking leaves out of a rake. "Hey, Max how are you doing?" Jim asked.

"Pretty good. Just bored. My dad has me raking the grass clippings and leaves into the gutter. Some fun huh? What are you up to?"

Jim acted like he was taking a casual walk. "Oh kind of a quiet day. Watched some boats at the river, broke a few pop bottles at the ball field, and got arrested."

Max did a double take, "What arrest..." Max tried to ask but was interrupted.

"Hey Max, this is my friend, Dave Nelson. He's from Jefferson and wrestles. I'll bet he can pin you here on the lawn even though you outweigh him by some fifty pounds or more."

Max and I both were confused. He was wondering about the arrest and I was wondering why Jim wanted me to wrestle a huge kid I'd just met. That beating from my old man was looking better and better.

Max looked bewildered, "What do you mean wrestle? I don't wrestle. Why would we do that? No offense but Dave is a little guy and I wouldn't want to hurt him."

"Little and hurt me" were the only words I heard. This guy didn't know who he just ticked off and he was mine.

I squatted down, shifted my body to the right and then to the left with my right arm partially extended and my left hand near my chest. I peered into his eyes to show no respect and no fear. His posture stiffened and I noticed his leg out to the side. He did not have a clue for what was coming next. I made a couple swipes with my right hand as I slid to the grass and snatched his left leg throwing him to the ground with a single leg take down. He rolled over on his stomach, gave out a groan and tried to stand. I grabbed his right arm and put him in the Hawaiian sling shoving him back into the lawn. I jumped to his side and gave him a chicken wing rolling him to his back. To polish him off, I wrapped his nearest leg in mine and pressed my chest into his as hard as I could.

"I give! I give," he yelled.

I rose to my feet picking up my T-shirt and wiped the grass off my sweaty body. Max sat halfway up and stared at me. "That was great. How'd you do that to me?"

"See? I told you so. This guy here is a pretty good wrestler on the team at Jeff," Jim told him. "You should try going out for it sometime."

It was almost fifty years later and I heard the full story of Max and his success at wrestling. He began wrestling because of that summer afternoon on Shiras in his front lawn. Years later he won the heavyweight division for Iowa High School representing

Wahlert High School in Dubuque. Apparently he told a friend how he came to enjoy the sport. He said he was intrigued how the little kid pinned him on his back in his own front yard years before.

If we'd not been caught breaking pop bottles, I may never have met Max. He might never have wrestled. There are reasons for things in life. So I can honestly say I once pinned the heavy weight Iowa State Wrestling Champ. I just won't tell the entire truth.

Three of the best wrestling programs in America are located in Iowa. They are The University of Iowa, Iowa State University, and The University of Northern Iowa. Dan Gable is America's best wrestler in the history of the sport. He coached at the University of Iowa for many years. His prep and college record was 182-1. He was undefeated as a prep wrestler and 118-1 while wrestling for Iowa State University. He was three-time all-American and three time Big Eight Champion.

David Nelson Nelson

"Gems and Thefts"

Each of us has experienced a moment in time when we met someone unforgettable, someone that we'd never forget. It was that way with Rex, Veronica, Tom, Jim, and Kosta. It was also that way with Jane.

To be exact, it was Mrs. Jane Reid. She was our guidance counselor during all three grades at Jeff. We had the honor and privilege of attending her class one semester each year. She impressed all of us, and that fact alone was huge. Why, she even pronounced Kosta's last name correctly the first day and that impressed him. She was the only teacher to pronounce it correctly and that was the only class where Kosta did not fall asleep. She respected us and we all felt like she was our friend. In turn, we respected her and agreed she was the best teacher at Jeff.

Mrs. Reid came to Jeff after teaching English at Fulton Elementary School. Veronica already knew her and she and Mrs. Reid were on good terms. At Jefferson she was responsible for "guiding" some of the worst miscreants in all of Dubuque. She was the most impressive teacher I think I ever had in school.

It wasn't her dress that consisted of the latest in fashions or her expensive jewelry that complimented her black hair. It was the way she carried herself. She was the first person we ever saw who wore eyeglasses on a chain around her neck. If she left the room for a moment, we could always hear the clickety-click of her high heels coming back toward us.

Mrs. Reid taught us simple, yet foreign customs. We learned that when you eat soup or any other liquid, you always glide the spoon away from yourself. We were taught never to have an arm resting on the dinner table when we ate. She must have worn out her long nails tapping them into the backs of thousands of kids over the years to remind them to sit up straight. She taught us that a sign of confidence was a firm handshake and straight posture. We

PALS: Part One

learned how to correctly fill out forms and print legibly. I remember those lessons even today and use what I learned so long ago. I imagine each of you had at least one teacher you remember, but nobody could compare to Mrs. Reid.

I was cautious. Always cautious. I always wondered if Mrs. Reid would attack me as so many other adults did back then. She was the person we had to see before eighth period penalties. That was our detention time. She required us to sit in her office and tell her everything that happened. She was firm and she was fair. Mrs. Reid treated everyone the same and she never belittled anyone. She taught us to believe in ourselves – or at least try.

In the seventh grade we had to write our autobiography. She then used her free time to meet with each of us one on one. I couldn't tell the truth so I lied.

Instead, I told her how everything was great in my life. But the looks she gave me indicated she knew differently and she told me I had a lot to give to others. I remember leaving her office cautiously optimistic that finally some adult of authority could and possibly would respect me.

By the ninth grade there was respect that went both ways. Nightly phone conversations with Veronica helped me to open those secret doors and to begin to share my feelings. After we took our aptitude tests, Mrs. Reid said she was impressed with my potential. I finally found an adult whom I could trust and share my feelings.

Unfortunately, ninth grade was the most stressful time for me as a youngster. I am not certain if it was rage against others or just being fourteen years old. I was in a bad place.

Take my friend Rich for example. Most nights it was, "Hey, are we on for tonight?"

"Yeah sure," I answered. "I have to sneak out but I'll be there."

David Nelson Nelson

Rich was a kid I did not hang around with much as he was not in the Boy's Chorus, did not wrestle, play football or run track like I did. He too was from an abusive alcoholic home and left to run the streets of the North End. He wore his long black hair with a "duck's ass" in the back that he kept in line with Brylcream. Naturally, he always had a black plastic comb popping out of his left back pocket. He kept his Salem cigarettes rolled up inside the left sleeve on his white T-shirt.

A few days earlier he'd told me about seeing a parked bulldozer at Linwood Cemetery and asked if I wanted to steal it with him. I'm not certain if I wanted to be accepted by this "hood" or if it was the excitement of it all, but I said yes. And the plan was made. We agreed to meet one Friday night late and steal the heavy equipment.

On warm spring or cool summer evenings, Ma and Dad sat outside at night drinking next to the two lilac bushes. Other than the lit candles used to combat mosquitos, there was no light.

From my bedroom above I heard the television in the kitchen and knew Dad was drinking. I knew I could sneak away after making a "dummy" under the covers. I was an expert in this field. My dummy was better than any scarecrow Hollywood could devise. I pried the window open and proceeded to sidestep my way to the drainpipe some twelve-feet away. My toes clung to the near-rotted trim that creaked with each shift of my weight. My fingertips grasped the underside of the other windows as I moved toward the corner drainpipe. I was halfway there when I heard, "What the hell are you doing?"

I froze on the ledge, my nose pressed against a window. I spoke not a word. I was as silent as a bat. My heart was racing wildly, sweat was dripping from the ends of my hair onto both hands, and I was afraid I might fall. My toes and fingertips started to cramp from the static position.

Again I heard, "You stupid son-of-a-bitch, what are you doing up there?"

"Me?" I asked.

"Alright I've had enough of this shit," he said as I heard the kitchen screen door slam beneath me.

As quickly as I could I wiggled my way back to the open window and jumped into bed like I was asleep. My skillful maneuvers did not fool him. After all, I had just spoken words from the ledge. I knew what was coming and my dad didn't disappoint me. I was whipped and punched for trying to sneak out of the house.

When I returned to school that Monday, I was actually glad for the deserved whipping I received. Rich apparently had stolen the heavy equipment and drove it over several headstones and through a gate. Somehow he managed to roll it over in a ditch and was saved when he jumped off in the process. He was caught and arrested. There was talk of him being sent to Eldora Reformatory for delinquent boys.

"What happened to your face?" Mrs. Reid asked me later in the day.

"I got hit by a baseball right in the cheek, and…"

She tried to make contact with my eyes as I looked at the floor. She placed her hand on my shoulder and gave me a gentle squeeze. "Come into my office. Now, Dave I thought you trusted me. I thought you felt safe with me. I know you are lying and there is nothing I can do about your home life, but never lie to me again."

I just nodded my head in agreement and left her office. It was six weeks later when the final shoe dropped. I was making toast for breakfast when Rich knocked at the back door. I opened it and he said, "Come on let's go. Kevin stole his Dad's car and we're going for a ride."

Going out the door, the last thing I remembered as I grabbed my jacket was the toast popping up. There we were, three fourteen-year old kids riding in a stolen car. The excitement was incredible.

That's not what Veronica felt though when Mrs. Reid called her into the office and told her what was happening. It had not taken long for Kevin's Dad to call the cops. They in turn called the school. We didn't have a clue.

We were out of town as fast as we could go without a care in the world. We were headed towards Manchester, Iowa. At one point Rich dared Kevin to see if he could do over 100 miles per hour He did. The car was shaking and rattling down that highway. It must have looked like I had a grin on my face, but in reality, it was pure terror that we might get in an accident.

Later that day, common sense told us we were in trouble. The three of us decided to go to school and face the music. We pulled to the curb and Rich and I got out. Kevin stayed behind the wheel.

"Aren't you coming into school," I asked.

"Nope. I'm headed off for better things."

And just like that, he drove away. That was the last I saw of him until three years later. I was getting ready to run the finals of the 100-yard dash at the Drake Relays in Des Moines. I heard someone yell my name and dang if it wasn't Kevin there on a field trip with the State Home for Juvenile Delinquents. He had been locked up all that time after being caught in Kansas stealing cars. And probably would still be stealing cars if he hadn't been caught.

Back at school, and that day several teachers and the principal met us at the front doors. Mrs. Reid said she would handle me and led me to her office. "Sit right there, Mister," she commanded as she pointed to the chair in her office. What hurt more than anything, was how she kept avoiding my eyes.

She leaned forward in her chair and tapped her pencil on the desk and said five words that crushed me, absolutely did me in.

"I am ashamed of you!"

And then she walked out her office door, and was gone for thirty minutes. I sat there thinking the entire time about what I'd done, and how I'd do things differently if I had a chance. When she returned I saw her jaw muscles moving and her face was bright red. Again, she refused to look at me in the eye. With an outstretched arm and pointed finger, I heard, "Get out of my office – NOW!"

I was crushed. I was ashamed. I was alone.

Veronica refused to answer her phone for many nights after that happened. Rex shunned me, as he knew we had a track meet coming up and they needed me. He figured the principal would not allow me to participate. I was allowed to run in that meet the following week because the coach arranged special punishment. He made me run many extra laps around the track for the next ten practices.

The most bizarre thing occurred that night when I went home. Nothing. That's correct. Not a word was said. Not a fist was raised. No type of physical abuse that night at home could have hurt more than the disappointment I caused "with" my friends and Mrs. Reid. After that, I felt things between us were never the same.

I didn't learn until a few decades later that it was Coach Udelhoff and Mrs. Reid who were instrumental in my earning a Track & Field scholarship at the University of Dubuque.

David Nelson Nelson

"Auto Theft and Bombs"

"Hey ya dork, get your butt upstairs and stop working on your model car. I have a surprise for you," I yelled down the basement steps to Tom as I stood in the kitchen doorway at his house.

I almost felt the scraping of his metal stool against the cement floor below and knew he heard my command. I was in the empty living room and knew the two of us were alone in the house. His dad's car was gone and his sisters were nowhere to be seen.

Tom looked shocked and said, "What the heck are those? Are those bullets?"

"Yeah, I stole 'em from my Uncle Clem. I've got a great idea I saw in a movie."

Tom giggled his devilish laugh. "Oh God, why don't I like this idea already?"

"How'd you like to make a bomb?" I studied his face and could tell he was on board by his big grin.

He leaned across me and touched the bullets with his index finger. "A bomb. How can we do that?"

"Easy. Here's what we do. We take toilet paper and wrap each bullet into a wad of it. Then we wrap all the wads together into one big clump. Using one of your old socks we put all the bullets into the sock and soak it with lighter fluid. We'll set the bomb across the street on the railroad tracks, turn off all the lights and see what happens."

He darted up the stairs to the bathroom and yelled over his shoulder, "Oh this'll be great. Ma and Dad won't be home for hours and my sisters are both working. I love it."

Moments later we were busy at the kitchen table creating our masterpiece like a couple of commandoes from WWII. There were seventeen bullets. The box labeled them as "twenty-two long rifle." We had no idea what that meant, but we knew this was going to work.

"Wait a minute. We have to really saturate the sock now," I scolded, as he wanted to light it before it was complete. We were soaking the sock in the dark while standing on the railroad tracks. We looked both ways to be certain nobody was driving up Kniest Street. When it was time, we laid the bomb on the tracks and lit it. There was quite the glow and we raced across the street and into the safety of Tom's living room.

All the lights were off and we peered through the partially opened blinds. At first our homemade bomb just seemed to burn down and then smolder. "How long 'till it explodes?" Tom asked.

I shrugged my shoulders. "I don't have a clue."

All of a sudden we heard a ping and a pop and watched the sock jump up and seem to explode. We laughed, held our breath, and laughed some more. Not all of the bullets erupted at the same time. It seemed to take several minutes between explosions. There we were having the time of our lives when we noticed the lights of an oncoming car.

My heart raced with excitement. "Oh crap. I hope none of them go off when that car goes by."

"Oh nuts. It's Marty. We have to get him in the house so he doesn't get hit by one." Tom ran to the door, stuck his head outside and said with a loud whisper, "Marty get in here. Hurry. Get in here."

Just as he closed the front door, a loud, 'POW' was heard.

Marty jumped like he was shot and looked over his left shoulder. "What the heck was that?"

Marty was the husband of Tom's oldest sister. He was so laid back and moved so slow he could walk all day in a wheelbarrow and never have to turn around. To watch him leap those steps two at a time was something neither of us had ever seen. He was several years older than us and always liked to hear about our latest adventures. Tonight he was in the middle of one.

All three of us watched with excitement as the sock jumped and flipped around on the tracks bursting with new explosions. After what seemed like an hour everything grew quiet. It was not until the next day we realized one of those bullets could have gone into someone's window. But they didn't and even if they had there were lots of kids in the neighborhood to blame.

It was a couple years later when Tom's sister and Marty were married and moved to Bettendorf, Iowa. Several times we were invited to spend the weekends with them. Now being two clever thinking teenagers, we came up with an idea. We would steal Marty's car after they fell asleep.

Tom moved quietly like a cat. "OK, I got his keys. He left them on the coffee table again. Let's go," Tom whispered as he poked me and squeezed the keys together with his hand to prevent any jingling.

Despite trying our best to be quiet, the creaking of the front door on the mobile home was magnified by our adrenaline rush. We snuck out the door on our toes to the waiting 1965 Chevy Chevelle. Tom opened the front door an inch at a time, put the car in neutral, and grabbed the steering wheel while standing on the outside. I was in the back and the two of us began to push. All that was heard was the crunching gravel under the tires of the slow moving car. We rolled it about seventy-five yards down a slight hill and stopped. With both of us inside, Tom started it up and away we went, at a whopping ten miles per hour. Once we knew the sound of the mufflers would not be heard, he gunned it and we were cruising. We were looking for chicks to pick up.

PALS: Part One

Now at three in the morning on a Monday, there were not many choices of girls. We weren't picky. We were horny teenagers and could have cared less what the girls looked like. As a matter of fact there were no choices. We drove probably a hundred miles that night around Davenport, Iowa, Moline, and East Moline, Illinois. It didn't matter as we enjoyed the music blaring and the warm summer evening air. I can still remember the song, "Ferry Cross The Mersey," sung by Gerry and the Pacemakers. We pretended to be older than our sixteen years. We never did get caught and for the life of me, I still wonder why Marty never noticed his gas gauge lower in the mornings.

David Nelson Nelson

"The Bridge Jump"

The water at the Municipal Swimming Pool offered relief from the hot, humid summer days. All of us had been there for at least three hours. We splashed every girl at least twice and dunked little kids until our shoulders were sore. We were ready for some different action.

Kosta hit my left shoulder with his fist. "Hey, I have an idea."

"What?"

"Let's go to the East Dubuque train bridge, jump off and go swimming at the sand bar."

"Aw, I don't think so," Rex replied. "That's pretty dangerous and a long way to walk."

"Walk, who said anything about walking?" Jim butted in.

"Well, we sure can't hitchhike so how are we getting there?"

"We hop a flat car when the train comes by," Kosta said. "The train has to slow down at the far end of town and then it's just a few miles to the bridge." He looked at each of us in the eyes waiting or a response. "Who's up for it?"

Everyone agreed it would be a great way to end the day. Well, nearly everyone. Rex was hesitant until we reminded him there would be older girls at the sandbar. In a flash, he was the first one out of the pool area and into the changing rooms.

Iowa and Illinois are connected with a train bridge that was constructed in the 1800s. It sits about fifty-feet above the powerful channel of the Mississippi River and allows for rail commerce to travel in in both directions. The bridge opens in the middle to allow barges and other river traffic to pass through. There's a bridge tender that sits in a "shack" as we called it, mid-way across the bridge. The tender opens and closes the center section with controls located inside his shack. On the southern side of the bridge is a gangplank about two feet wide. It's located beneath the rails and off to the side. In case a train is coming, workers use the plank for a place of safety.

The five of us walked the tracks waiting for the next train. We played a game of trying to see who could walk the farthest on the rails without falling. When that became dull we sang songs. Mostly, they were disgusting, dirty tunes we learned from older kids. It was about halfway to the Pack when we heard the train coming from the north and scattered like ants as we dove into the high grass alongside the tracks. We hid until the engine was at least seventy-five yards away so we wouldn't be seen by the engineer.

Kosta looked back at us. "Hurry up, run faster."

"Oh, God, this is too funny," I said as I sprinted to the front of the group, threw my towel on the flat car, grabbed the steel handle and jumped on. "Hurry up you bunch of pansies," I yelled.

Kosta was next to hop on, followed by Jim, who was laughing with excitement. Tom was long-legged and had no trouble flipping himself off the steps and onto the flat car. Rex was running and holding on to the side of the car, his feet slipping on the gravel, and he had a look of terror on his face.

We felt the train begin to pick up speed. "Hurry up, you dick head." Kosta screamed. "Run faster, you only have a little further to go."

In what seemed like a half mile, Rex was finally on board and about to puke his guts out while on all fours. After a few moments we heard all kinds of cussing from him. We looked at one another and said, "Pussy."

Rex was a fast sprinter. The speed of the train was not his concern. He told us later it was jumping up on to the steps that frightened him. The train slowed to a crawl in the manufacturing area of Dubuque. After hopping off near the Dubuque Star Brewery we quickened our pace toward the train bridge. Conversations increased in tempo as adrenaline filled our arteries.

"Here's how I see it," Kosta said. "I'll go first because I've done it before. Everyone follow my lead. Rex you go behind me."

Rex came to a sudden stop. "Oh crap. I don't know if I can do this. What happens if we get caught?"

Jim laughed. "Well the last kids who got caught were sent to a reform school."

Rex waived his right arm back and forth. "I'm not going. My old man will kill me for sure."

"Jim, knock it off. That's not true. He's pulling your leg. The worst thing that will happen is that we get carded by the cops. Even that's no big deal," I said.

While Rex called Jim a bastard, Kosta went on to explain. "Look, if the bridge tender comes out either run like hell to the far end and jump into the channel, or just jump where you are. One way or another we're going into that river."

"And what the heck am I suppose to do with my glasses?" Tom asked.

"Well you're up a shit crick without a paddle," Jim laughed.

"No, he's up a river without a paddle," I chimed in and four of us chuckled while Tom stuck his glasses into his back pocket.

Kosta pointed at me. "Dave, you're the fastest, so you go last. That way if we are seen and have to run, you can out-run the guy and just jump in."

Within minutes we were on the gangplank crawling our way fifty feet over the most powerful river in the world. Moments

PALS: Part One

before we had been sweating from the terrible Iowa humidity and heat of the day. Now the winds cooled us and blew drips of sweat into the channel below. To my right I could see specks of kids at the East Dubuque sandbar and cars passing over the Illinois Bridge.

An eerie quiet fell over us. There wasn't any kidding now. There was no conversation at all. Even if there were, none of us could have been heard over the whooshing wind doing its thing with our minds. We were scared. We were focused. We were on a mission. I noticed a tree being pushed down river and wondered for a second what might happen if we hit debris in the channel. My sudden attack of cotton mouth made it impossible to swallow. It was too late and there was no turning back.

"Hurry up, Dave. He's coming. Run!" I heard somebody say as I changed gears and went into my Jesse Owens speed the best I could on the tracks. I saw Kosta jump, followed by Rex and then Tom holding his glasses. Jim was yelling at me up to the very end. He was the only one to dive into the river. I looked over my shoulder to see where the tender was and saw he had no chance of stopping me. I made my turn facing the river square and jumped without hesitation.

I hit the water in what seemed like eighty-miles an hour. I remembered thinking how fun it was and also how cold it was. The farther I sank, the blacker it became. OK, I can stop going down anytime now, I thought.

I had no control. It took all my strength to rise to the surface. The river's current pushed me as if I were a twig. With all my effort, I made two strokes of the American Crawl and hit the sand bar some quarter-mile from where we jumped. There was backslapping, laughing, shoving, and congratulatory comments from older kids. But none of that mattered to Rex. He was already telling some girls from Senior High School how he did this all the time. They were, to say the least, impressed.

David Nelson Nelson

"The Spring Thaw"

When the Mississippi River froze, avid fishermen would cut holes in the ice and fish. Some would sit on stools covered head to toe seeking protection from the below zero temperature. Smarter ones would hide inside solar tents to get out of the wind. My brother, Richard fished this way. I never thought any of those people were normal. What fun was that?

My buddies and I had a different form of wintery entertainment on the river. Kosta came up with a bright idea to walk across the Mississippi River now that it was beginning to thaw.

Kosta baited us with a challenge. "Aw, you chickens. That's the fun of it – to see if we can walk over and get back in one piece."

"Wait a minute," I said. "Have you ever done this before?"

"No, but I sure have thought about it enough. Where's your spirit, Nelson? I can't believe you are such a wimp," he said teasingly.

"All right, I'm in. Nobody calls me a wimp," I said and left the table at Riverside Bowling Lanes to get another pop.

As I walked away I heard Kosta, Tom, Jim, and Rex in unison repeating, "Wimp, wimp, wimp."

I just smiled to myself and knew we were going to do this.

When I returned Jim asked, "Hey, Nelson do you think we should call the police department and ask Barney Fife if this is OK to do?"

I was going to make a comment but was interrupted by Tom, "Hey look, look, look, it's going to cover my pop glass."

He was referring to a smoke ring Kosta just blew across the table. Rex covered his nose and mouth with his left hand and then fanned the perfect ring away with his other hand.

Kosta grinned. "Schweikert, you're easily amused."

"You want amusement, I'll show you how I can light a fart," he cackled.

Rex covered his nose with the palm of his hand. "Spare us, please. If yours are anything at all like Jim's I'm running away."

"Oh yeah," Jim said, "Who's the one who farts to music?"

Kosta let out a long laugh. "I'll tell you what, if the ice isn't thawing yet, I'll pee a hole in it. *Then* it'll start to crack."

"Yeah, with your ability to pee and Tom's ability to light farts, one way or another, we're going to see some melted ice," I said.

We left the bowling lanes and walked past Municipal Pool and north towards the dam. We discussed the frequent topic of the pros and cons of dating Catholic girls versus non-Catholic one. We decided the non-Catholic girls were more fun because we didn't need to pretend to be religious to get into their bras. We followed the tracks further north and passed Flat Rock. About a half-mile above the dam we slid down the bank over frozen dead weeds and then we were standing on partially frozen ice.

"OK, Here we go. Look for any wet spots. It's kind of like when Nelson pees the bed," he said while all the others hooted with laughter.

I just shook my head and ignored the attempt at humiliation. I was not about to die on this venture and was instead getting myself focused. The river was about three quarters of a mile wide between Iowa and Wisconsin. We decided to walk at an angle so we could cover more territory.

There'd been many more warm days than cold ones in the previous ten days. Slush covered the sidewalks. A month earlier, those same sidewalks were solid with ice and snow. The river had small patches of snow and ice, but overall most of the snow had melted away. There were visible signs of thawing that could be seen from quite some distance. Open holes in the ice could be as large as twenty feet in diameter. There were also small openings that one does not see until coming close to it. That was the fun part.

Kosta took charge. "Everybody get into a semi-circle and walk together towards that hole. Let's see how close we get."

"Wait, I have a better idea, I said. "Let's see who is the last one is to chicken out. He gets a cigarette from all the others."

Rex cleared his throat, "I don't smoke, what am I supposed to do?"

"Steal some from your dad, you moron." Jim shouted as he ran and slid on the ice several feet away.

Tom yelled as he pushed his glasses up his nose with his left hand, squatted down, flattened his other hand on the ice and gazed north. "Oh crap. Did you hear that?"

He'd no sooner said that when we heard a sound like a rock going through a window at Audubon. Shattered ice ripped a hole that caused several shards to stick out of the river and water lapped up the chunks. Tom and Rex ran back some twenty-yards.

"If I am going to die, I want to do it when I'm smoking," I said as I lit a cigarette and then continued forward.

To my right, I saw the movement before I heard the ice break under Kosta's feet. He yelled out and somehow managed to keep his balance as the ice split. He jumped backwards and took off running in the direction of Rex and Tom. The ice continued to split. I heard laughter from the three of them but didn't understand what

PALS: Part One

they were saying. I was focused on winning some smokes from all of them.

The pieces that broke near Kosta weakened the spot near Jim. He put his hands over his heart and said, "OK, I give up. You win, Nelson."

Rapid chattering, laughter and no one listening to another went on for a couple minutes after we were safe. I remember thinking how fun this was and hit Kosta on the right shoulder. "That was great."

When river ice breaks, sometimes the sound can be heard from many miles away. The noise is like a train coupling its cars, but with a deep thunderous roll like a springtime storm. You can feel the power beneath your feet and sometimes echoing in your chest. That is what happed about mid-way across.

We all stopped dead in our tracks. Rex let out a whoop. "Whoa, what is that noise?"

"It must be the ice cracking somewhere," Kosta said as he cleared his left nostril.

Not a one of us spoke. We stood paralyzed looking north toward Minnesota. The thunderous rumble was coming closer, closer still. About a hundred-yards away a huge chunk of ice heaved upward and landed crooked on top of another piece. Through the middle of us, we saw the ice split into many lines and felt the fracturing deep into our chests. We were too frightened to move. Just then more ice split open fifty-yards behind us. That piece reminded me of a submarine coming up out of the water.

It was bigger than a car. It creaked, cracked, and shattered into several large chunks. It reminded me of the blocks of ice that were on the iceman's wagon. This time there would be no chipping off of pieces to suck the liquid out. Then there was quiet, silence. The ice thunder stopped.

David Nelson Nelson

All five of us collapsed our frozen postures and once again rattled in simultaneous conversation. Jim pointed out the area where we stood moments before had re-frozen. Initially the ice split and for some reason connected itself back together. There were obvious signs of melting the closer we approached the Wisconsin side of the river. We turned and headed back across to the Iowa side. We repeated the ice- breaking adventures many times, but not one was as exciting as the first one. Jeez, isn't that true of life in general?

"Put Out or Get Out"

Any kid growing up in Dubuque would tell you that the Mississippi River was a source of entertainment. It was a great place to swim, fish, and watch riverboats and barges going upstream or down river. I always enjoyed going to the lock and dam and to watch barges pass through the locks. People who gathered at Eagle Point Park often would enjoy the scene from their vantage point some 300 feet above.

Todd and I walked the boat docks near Municipal swimming pool. "Oh, God, here's one with the keys in it. Let's take it," Todd whispered to me.

I moved fast. Who could resist such temptation? "You drive and I'll get the ropes unhooked. Ah, this is going to be great. Hurry up, hurry up."

Todd was a Catholic kid who lived near Comisky Park. I didn't hang around with him much because we went to different schools but we did play on the same baseball team during the summer. He was a nice enough kid, but always seemed to get into trouble. That day I joined him and was swept away in the excitement of stealing a boat.

We were sputtering along in the *"No Wake Zone"* and acting like we owned the place. Once we were in the channel, Todd shifted into full gear and almost immediately we were shooting rooster tails in our wake.

I tried to light a cigarette in the wind. "Isn't this great." I hunkered down on the carpeted floor of the twenty-foot ski boat, lit two cigarettes and gave one to Todd. Our eyes were watering as we skimmed the water as fast as the forty-horsepower outboard motor could go. And then we pulled up and drifted in neutral near the Sixteenth Street Bridge.

Todd slapped the steering wheel with his opened right hand. "Hey, I just had a thought. Did you see those two girls swimming off the docks back there?"

"Yeah, so what's your point?"

"Let's see if they'll come with us. Everybody likes a boat ride. Maybe we can go to that island over there and make-out."

I flicked my cigarette into the water. "Oh wow, man, that's a great idea. Count me in."

Todd turned the wheel, once again pushed the lever forward and off we went at full speed. I looked behind at our wake and saw some guy giving us the finger. He was fishing under the bridge in a johnboat and we created quite a wake for him. With insouciance, I shot a bird in return and faced forward. I was scoping out the banks looking for the two girls.

"I guess we made that guy fishing back there kinda mad with our wake. He shot me a bird."

Todd swerved the boat to miss a log and we rocked left and right. "The hell with him."

Moments later, he dropped back into low gear as the river caught up with us and lifted and pushed our boat towards the docks. I spotted the first girl and waved and she, lucky girl that was about to be kissed by me, reciprocated.

"Hey, guys what are you two up to today," the blonde called out as she squeezed the water from her hair. Her head bent and turned toward us. She used both arms to dry her hair with her towel. I saw a bit of cleavage and knew she was the one for me.

"Hi. Do youse girls want to go for a ride in my boat?" Todd yelled over the rumble of the engine.

"Hey, don't I know you? Don't you go to Wahlert," the redhead said. "Aren't you a couple years behind me?"

Todd smiled for a moment. "Yeah, what grade are you in?"

"We're seniors," my new girlfriend said as she giggled into her hand and motioned to the other girl. "C'mon, Angie let's go riding."

As the girls walked toward the boat, I told Todd we should avoid the Sixteenth Street channel. That guy fishing might throw something at us. He nodded in agreement. I was sitting on the long back seat with Sharon while Angie was up front with Todd. He allowed Angie to drive the boat, but only if he could wrap his arms around her and also hold the wheel. I attempted idle chatter, but had never been with an older woman before and felt clumsy and awkward.

A half-mile or so below the Pack, Todd turned the boat toward the bank. With the boat in neutral, he spun Angie around and tried to kiss her. With that signal, I tried the same but my girl forcefully shoved me away. Todd laughed. "OK, girls put out or get out."

With that comment, both girls stood on the back seat and dove in. I received a well-deserved slap across my left cheek just before Sharon dove in. They swam to shore leaving one blue and one white bath towel behind. "The hell with 'em," Todd said as once again we shot a rooster tail and spun the boat in a circle several times. We headed up river and pulled into the rocky bank below the dock where thirty minutes earlier we'd picked up the two girls. He turned the boat off and we hit some big rocks on the bank and came to a halt. We got out and just left the boat banging against the rocks.

Walking together towards Municipal Pool, we laughed and joked about the fun and almost getting to make-out. Behind us, I saw the untethered boat floating down river towards the Sixteenth Street channel.

David Nelson Nelson

About two weeks later the doorbell rang. Naturally, it was the police. We were caught and charged with theft. I was placed on probation for one year and if I didn't get into more trouble, my record would be cleared. Once a month I had to meet with a probation officer and tell him what I did during the past month. I indeed stayed out of trouble, at least for that year. I never hung out with Todd again. It was not because of the boat incident. It was just another instance where people come and go in our lives like waves coming into the bank on the river's edge and back out again.

I never received any punishment at home for the incident. I was not beaten, I was not grounded (where I was confined to the yard and house), and I was not even scolded. That was one time I expected to be pulverized. I never questioned "why."

PALS: Part One

"On My Honor"

Immanuel Congregational United Church located at 1795 Jackson Street was the home for our Boy Scout Troop. My brother, Richard and I were members together. The previous few years I was active in Cub Scouts and Weblos. Tom and I were in the same Cub Pack, but he didn't want to become a Boy Scout. He preferred melting model cars.

One of the best parts of Cub Scouts was the Pinewood Derby. We were each given a wooden block of pine, wheels, and axles. My dad helped me design and create a car and he did most of the work. I didn't care that I was eliminated at the Derby. It was fun that we had done this together. Sadly, I don't remember much of that positive process and the event itself. I can remember in greater detail the various forms of punishment and abuse I received from him. I suppose I'm hard-wired to remember negative events more so than positive.

Boy Scouts was a positive experience for me. I earned three Merit Badges before quitting about two years later. I regret that now, but at the time I was more interested in girls and was too busy with wrestling, track & field, and just hanging around. One merit badge was for First Aid, another for Hiking, and the last was Citizenship. Now there is a hoot – me, David Nelson Nelson earning a citizenship badge.

The reason I liked scouting was because there were rules and procedures to follow. There were exact methods on how to dress, the exact way to salute, the best way to pitch a tent, and even make a campfire. I liked knowing the rules and trying to follow them. I enjoyed watching boys receive their Eagle Badges. That was the highest achievement in scouting. I also liked to fart inside the tent and see if I could make my partner puke. None ever did, but boy they sure came close. I wish they'd given merit badges for that activity.

David Nelson Nelson

Richard was my hero. Since we were small children, he had set the gold standard of doing what was right regarding correct behavior. I tested new waters at every opportunity, while he led a straight and narrow path. As part of our hiking merit badge, we had to hike five ten-mile hikes and one twenty-mile. Three of us hiked from Dubuque to our Scout Master's cabin on the river in Bellevue, Iowa for the twenty-mile hike. It was tough for young kids. About half way through I suggested we hitch hike. My theory was that it was also considered a hike because both methods contained the word "hike." Richard said he would tell on me if I cheated and I knew he was right, I followed his lead and was glad I did because the sense of accomplishment taught me that sometimes things that are tough could be overcome.

He and I wanted to attend Camp Klaus Boy Scout Camp in Greeley, Iowa. Our parents didn't have the twenty-dollars each for the admission fee. We were told that if we each collected at least one ton of newspapers, John Deere would pay us twenty dollars per ton. They in turn used the papers for packing material.

Dad cleaned out the garage so we could store the papers. He told us he would take the loads to John Deere in the family station wagon. Richard and I had one wagon and had to share it going door to door, collecting the papers. We set scheduled days where each of us had the wagon to haul our loads. I can remember asking people in the North End if they would save their papers for me. Veronica even offered to help and asked several people in her area to save papers for me. Many a cold, rainy night I would pull the wagon and walk a few miles loaded down with my "stash." It took us weeks, then months to collect a ton of papers. We were required to tie each stack in twenty-five pound bundles. Within that time, the entire garage was filled. It was exciting to see our progress, and even more exciting when we received the twenty dollars for our hard work.

I also sold Salvo Salve to the women in my neighborhood. Mrs. Cierney and Mrs. Johnson bought at least ten tins of the product. I no longer remember what the product was used for, but it must have been pretty effective. I probably lied about what the product could do for folks. And finally, I'd made enough for spending money at Camp Klaus. I suspect Scouting contributed to my work ethic and I suspect that was another reason I liked the Scouts so much.

We earned our way to scout camp. Each day there were activities relating to the outdoors. We had to identify plants, bugs, and trees. One day our Troop built a bridge. Richard was the foreman of the project and at the week's end we were recognized for our bridge skills. The top honor went to me though. I was recognized by my troop as the best farter.

Boy Scout Oath
On my honor I will do my best
To do my duty to God and my country and to obey the Scout law;
To help other people at all times;
To keep myself physically strong, mentally alert and morally straight.

David Nelson Nelson

"Phocomelia"

I've always been comfortable with the elderly. As a physical therapist, I enjoyed and took great satisfaction treating them. I enjoyed hearing their stories. Each of us has at least one good story to tell. I think I learned this around age eight from Mrs. Cierney who lived two doors from us. She was one of these elderly folks I liked. She was born with a birth defect called Phocomelia. In her case, she had no legs – just two feet attached to her trunk. Despite this, she was able to propel herself in her wheelchair. If she was in a hurry, she would scoot herself into another room with her hands balancing herself with her rump. Little kids don't see the differences within others. I was like that.

When I was going to Audubon School, I used to sit and talk with her by the hour after school. I don't remember thinking she was odd or deformed. She was just a nice old lady who listened to a little boy.

Mrs. Cierney cared about me. She was always knitting something, sitting in her over-stuffed chair, and rolling a piece of thread around in her mouth. She wore a one-piece dress that was snug against her pudgy belly. She was soft-spoken, wore makeup every day, and her gray hair was always neatly brushed. She didn't have that old lady smell like my teachers at Audubon. On her left side was a table lamp where she kept the T.V. Guide, pencil and crossword puzzle book. The wooden decorative strips around the top of the table supported her large bag of multi-colored yarn and numerous needles poking out the top. Her home was always spotless. I'd sit on the davenport with my feet dangling several inches above the floor. When she spoke I'd prop my right arm on the armrest of the davenport, looked into her eyes and listened intently to her stories.

We sat and covered an array of topics. One time she told me her husband helped build the Golden Gate Bridge. That was interesting because we studied about the bridge one day and I told the rest of my class I knew somebody who helped build it. Neither

Miss Coffee nor my classmates believed me. That was not the first nor the last time people didn't believe something I said. I wondered why. Mrs. Cierney always wanted to know how I was doing in school and if I had any more ribbons from running in track. She told me one time that doing all my homework was important because she just knew I would amount to something good when I was older. What an intelligent and kind old lady she was.

I cut her lawn with our push-mower several times in order to help me receive my citizenship scouting merit badge. I would offer to pick up groceries at Huey's or Krammer's stores. Somewhere as I aged, I lost all contact with her. I'll bet she missed our chats, and it wasn't until I was older, that I realized I missed them too.

Sometimes in life all we have left are the stories and the memories. My patient, Bob Allen was like that. He reminded me of my childhood hours spent listening to Mrs. Cierny. Bob had been a pilot in WWII and he liked to tell me stories of his escapades. And I enjoyed hearing them. On his very first mission, Germans shot down his plane. There was one crewmember hit by bullets and had fallen unconscious. Other crewmembers asked then Captain Bob Allen what to do. As the plane was struggling to stay aloft, Bob told the crew to put a parachute on the unconscious crewman and throw him out. Bob figured the jolt might bring him back. If not, the guy was going to die either way. The plane was going to crash.

Floating down in his parachute, Bob said he saw a field full of German citizens armed with pitchforks and shotguns. In the distance he saw a car approaching with German soldiers and one civilian. They pulled into the field as Bob made his drop. The smartly dressed officer fired his pistol in the air and told the locals the prisoner was his. Bob was placed in the back of the convertible and driven around the town. The mayor sat next to him screaming at him the entire time. They showed Captain Allen the damage their bombs did to the community.

The next day he was brought in for questioning. The Germans knew where Bob lived in America, the name of their bombing mission, number of planes in the drop, and what their final targets

David Nelson Nelson

were for the mission. They also knew where Bob went to college, the number of children he had, and where he was born. They asked if there was anything else to add. He said "No", and was dismissed. He was never tortured. He remained a POW the rest of the war and was finally set free by General George Patton. That is what I mean when I say – everyone has a story. The injured airman who was thrown out of the plane did indeed live. After the war, he and Bob were friends for life.

Listening to Mrs.Cierney tell her interesting stories created an interest for me in what others have to say. From a young boy to present day, I've enjoyed the stories of others. That was one reason other patients of mine thought of me as a good physical therapist. I have great listening skills and I care about people. And lucky me, I have Mrs. Cierney to thank for that.

Upstairs from Mrs. Cierney lived a woman named Mrs. Johnson. She was the kind lady who allowed me to burn my camera project in the second grade in her burn barrel. I often heard arguments between her and her husband while knocking on her door. Then when she would open it for me to enter, all the arguing stopped when I went inside. I think she also enjoyed my visits. I would alternate spending time downstairs with Mrs. Cierney, or upstairs with Mrs. Johnson. I sat in Mrs. Johnson's kitchen telling tales about the limited events in my life.

I've always been a storyteller and I think it originated with these two ladies. I figured they had no way to confirm what I was saying, so I embellished. You would have thought I was the most magnificent little boy in the universe. One time I told Mrs. Johnson I made a hole in one while playing golf. She was so happy for me. The next week, Mrs. Cierney asked me how my golf game was coming along.

"What golf game? I don't play golf."

"Oh, Mrs. Johnson must have heard it wrong," she said.

PALS: Part One

Lesson One: A yarn or story is when you can repeat everything the same way more than once. A lie is when you cannot. I officially became a storyteller that year. I was in the sixth grade.

Two doors away from the ladies' house lived an eccentric old man whose apartment was in the basement of a large apartment house. Mr. Grant made violins by hand. He hung them overhead on hooks attached to the floor joists above. I never saw or noticed any people coming in or out of his two-room basement home. There were no pictures on his walls because they were made of fragile limestone that could not support such an item. His apartment was dark but always clean. He never spoke of his past or if he had a family somewhere. I don't remember ever seeing him outside during the day.

There were only three, very small, and dirty windows to see the lower legs and feet of a passerby on the sidewalk above. Some people walked with intention, little kids ran by on a mission, and many fathers staggered past the view from below. You can tell a lot looking at legs and feet. I would create stories in my mind about where they were going, but more importantly where they had been.

I had been in basements like Mr. Grant's all over our neighborhood. They were cool and damp in the summer and warm in the winter. The hardened linoleum flooring over the cement floor had a worn path in its center that went from his work space to the cast iron kitchen sink and off to the bathroom on the far end. There were two cupboards that sat on the floor next to a small kitchen table. The table had a white top with red trim on the sides. The metal chair legs had some early signs of rust. The two chair seats were covered with plastic. One had a couple splits in the side.

I never sat when I visited with Mr. Grant but stood at the work area where he always had pieces of wood clamped together on the workbench. Unlike chatting with the ladies, I didn't stay long and didn't share as much with him as I did with them. Richard had an interest in the viola and enjoyed hearing Mr. Grant talk about construction of the instruments. I never had the heart to tell Mr.

David Nelson Nelson

Grant I knew about the destruction of violins. Some things are better left unsaid.

Late at night I had a habit of sprinting past Audubon and the seven-foot high shrubs that separated it from Lincoln Avenue. The streetlights provided a sense of security. There was one light a block behind me, and another a block ahead. In between was a void of all things sane and sensible. I was frightened of the dark ever since Richard hid under our basement steps two years earlier in the potato bin. When I was going up the steps toward the kitchen light above, he reached between the steps and touched my leg. That contact along with his growl frightened me nearly to death. Lincoln Avenue was total darkness and I felt I was in our basement. The basement I feared sometimes.

Close to midnight on a windy, moonless, October night I was singing to myself and trotting up the street towards home from Tom's house. I was halfway up the block when I saw and smelled something that meant danger - for just a second before terror hit. I saw smoke drifting out from the shrubs and the glow of a cigarette. I immediately went into my Jesse Owens' sprint just as the fella yelled out.

"Rrrrr!" was immediately followed by laughter.

It was Mr. Grant. I knew his laugh. Wind blew the clanging metal cable on the flagpole ahead as an eerie "chink" sounded when I sprinted by. For a moment I thought Mr. Grant was behind me trying to grab my shoulder. I dashed the remaining block and leapt up the three cement steps leading into our front door. I never again visited him.

"Getting Even"

Almost every Sunday after church I was invited to one of my friend's home for lunch. Dale's dad was a minister and taught classes at Wartburg Seminary. It was Dale who wrestled at Senior High School on the varsity team in ninth grade along with me. He was one weight class above me. He and I would collect rocks or just hike around in the woods behind his house after church lunch. One particular Sunday, we had a bag full of rocks that we were planning to clean and categorize. Twin brothers approached us carrying a BB gun. They must have sensed I was afraid of them because they had no reservation about shooting the bag I carried in my hand. I said nothing. I did nothing. But I promised myself that someday I would get even with the one doing the shooting.

Several years later at the beginning of a wrestling match between the two junior high schools, that kid and I met in the middle of the mat to shake hands. And whammo, a light went off. It was that jerk who had shot my bag of rocks long before. I was dominant during our match. I knew I could pin him, but I wanted him to pay for what he'd done to me. I used the maneuver called the "Hawaiian Sling." This is a move where you pull the opponent's arm between his legs, grab his wrist and apply pressure on the gonads. He complained at each break, "Hey Ref, the guy is pulling my nuts."

I just smiled and dug my chin into his upper back. I used a "Half-Nelson" several times. Using a double leg takedown, I had no difficulty earning points. Finally I rolled him over and pinned his back and shoulders to the mat. Revenge is mine, I thought. That surely came from the Bible. I figured I was following my strong Lutheran influence. In addition to having the church's blessing I had the support of Kosta. He too was a wrestler and an excellent one. I remember him laughing out loud and yelling from his seat along the mat, "Go get him, Dave. Hurt him good."

It was comforting to have both God and Kosta on my side. I couldn't lose.

Only one thing bothered me throughout the entire match. The kid didn't remember me.

Strangely enough, once he was off my enemy list, he and I became friends. We enjoyed jokes, had passion for girls and saw humor in ways that others didn't. We went to high school and college together. We always met for a beer when I returned to Dubuque and often would go for a ride on the river in his boat. I was with him the night I met my future wife at the Brass Ring Restaurant and Bar. We are still friends to this day. Hallelujah! Pass the green Jello with tiny marshmallows on top.

"Shoes & Pews"

I had many jobs during my teenage years. I worked for Bob Ruegnitz who owned a drugstore with the same name. I made deliveries walking the neighborhood carrying bags of prescriptions. I cleaned the store, and matched various sized prescription bottles to their lids.

I picked strawberries, shoveled snow, cut lawns, and was a laborer for a brick mason. I sold Cutco Cutlery and Amway door to door. Amway sold a shoe spray product and an oven cleaner. I met with the head nun at Clarke College to promote my wares. The nuns had to have clean shoes and I figured clean ovens in the convent. She purchased a case of shoe spray several times. I put in a bid with the Dubuque County School District for selling floor wax in five gallon buckets. I did not get the bid, but like Babe Ruth I swung the bat. I was sixteen years old.

The most unusual job was conducted on a per diem basis. I was a professional pallbearer for a funeral home. A friend's aunt owned the place on Central Avenue. When there were no young people in a family, several of us were hired to carry the casket. Before the service we had to sit on a smaller version of a church pew. It held the six of us guys and we were required to be reverent (one of the Scout Laws). I earned twenty-dollars for each dead person I carried to the grave.

The most frustrating job I ever had was a ladies' shoe salesman at Stampfer's Department Store in Dubuque. I was paid a small salary and commission. It was not unusual to haul out ten boxes of size 4AA shoes, help the lady put them on, and then be rejected. I might have spent over thirty-minutes and then no sale. Little did I know that many years later I would be helping little old ladies in nursing homes put their shoes on so I could take them to physical therapy.

My dad, brothers, and I did a lot of work for my wealthy uncle. Clem Maguire lived at 275 Wartburg Place, which was across the street from Wartburg Seminary. His back yard bordered one of the golf fairways at the Country Club. He had married Ma's sister and was a devoted Catholic and Irish. Dad was hired to perform all types of odd jobs that included plumbing, electrical, and anything mechanical. He always paid Dad cash and then would come up with at least one other job before he left the house and after he was paid. That job became gratis and upset my parents, as they cussed him all the way across town to our neighborhood. My brothers and I worked cutting grass and shoveling snow for Uncle Clem.

Clem never did any work. He did, however, walk funny. He had an artificial leg, a prosthesis. Long-time Dubuquers knew him as "Peg" Maguire. He was a man of great wealth. He travelled the world and I liked hearing his stories when he returned. Clem was also quite the artist. One time he painted a portrait of Pope John the 23rd. He took that painting with him when he visited the Vatican and donated it. That was the year he was blessed by the Pope. For him it was a big deal. For us non-Catholics it meant nothing. Clem owned most of lower Main Street in Dubuque. While I can't prove it, rumor has it that he was a bootlegger for Al Capone. Word also had it that he was responsible for the tri-state areas of Illinois, Iowa, and Wisconsin.

One time on Good Friday I was hired to shovel snow off his driveway and sidewalk. I arrived late because I stopped to talk with one of Veronica's friends who lived several doors away. At 12:30 P.M. I was beginning my task. He came out cussing because I started to work. There was no work done in Dubuque by Catholics from noon until three in the afternoon on Good Friday. I always wondered who determined that time and was it Eastern or Central Time Zones that Jesus died? The screaming and cussing by a one-legged, wealthy, Irish Catholic toward a defenseless, poor, little German, Lutheran boy was too much for me to bear. Like a singer in the Alps that cold Friday afternoon, I dropped the shovel where I stood and began to sing in my soprano voice. *"A mighty fortress is our God, A Bulwark never failing. For still our ancient foe doth seek to work us woe."*

Martin Luther himself would have been proud of me. Until three in the afternoon I sat on Clem's wrought iron patio furniture waiting to begin my chore. He made me a treat of green Jello with marshmallows and brought it out to me. That was nice. Once again I had the blessing of God. I am thankful Kosta was not there. I don't think there would have been any treats. Kosta would have told the old guy to "stick-it."

I received no money from my parents for college. It was Uncle Clem who loaned me twenty-dollars for a dormitory deposit. I had to sign a promissory note and re-paid it with interest. When Clem died he left a sizeable amount to Loras College in Dubuque. His name is still known in the archives at that Catholic school.

Clem had a brother named Charlie. I was hired to sit with Charlie all night at the hospital. He was in and out of consciousness. I just sat there in the semi-dark room. He died shortly after I began that job. That was my first foray with the sick. I liked old people then and now.

Scout Law
A Scout is trustworthy, loyal, helpful, friendly, courteous, kind, obedient, cheerful, thrifty, brave, clean, and reverent.

David Nelson Nelson

"Preparing for Departure"

Veronica, Rex, Jim, Kosta, and I, along with all of our classmates received an excellent education at Jefferson Junior High School. Rex, Jim, Kosta, and I played football. Kosta and I wrestled while Jim and Rex were excellent basketball players. All of us ran track and I still see Tom's waving coal-black hair flopping left and right in the 440-yard relay. Rex was a speedster and great in the broad jump (I'll bet he knew the origin of the Maypole Dance – broad jump). Rex, Veronica, and I were on the Student Council. Rex and Veronica were in band. The three of us were in choral music together. I set a couple records in the fifty-yard and one hundred-yard dash that held up for several decades.

Rex and I would meet in the summer and workout trying to stay in shape for the upcoming year. I distinctly remember one afternoon we finished the lunch his mom provided and went into his yard. We lay under the shade of the pear tree. Looking up at the fruit and chewing on blades of grass, we discussed our goals and aspirations for what seemed like an hour. Rex was someone I tried to emulate. He was a role model for what was right, just like Richard.

Veronica was there at every sporting event to support us guys. My parents never attended any school function. They never saw me run, wrestle, or play football. Veronica and Rex made every honor roll. I squeaked by with average grades, as did Kosta and Jim. Despite my help with his homework, Tom didn't enjoy school. He quit after ninth grade and went to work. He did receive his GED years later. I am proud of him for achieving that goal.

During the time we were in school there were two nationally normed tests given to children across America. These tests were developed in Iowa. For children in the elementary level the test was called The Iowa Test of Basic Skills. At the junior and senior high levels the test was named the Iowa Test of Educational Development. Both tests were given to students across America, and normed nationally so the student's ranking could be compared locally, by state, or nationally. At the time of this writing, there is no normed national test and what is given may not be normed at all. What gets tested in one state is not necessarily tested in another.

In the ninth grade Kosta achieved one of the highest scores possible on the Iowa Test of Educational Development. Another student was handing out the test results and had the privilege of seeing all students' scores. She had the audacity to ask him, "How did you score so high, that's even better than mine. There must have been a mistake."

For those of us who lived in the Flats and other poor areas of the North End, that was a norm. Expectations for us were low. I think students from Jefferson were considered second-class compared to our cross-town rival junior high school. That school was where the wealthy kids attended. They were the ones most educators felt had the best potential. They were the children of professional parents who were active in the community. We were the sons and daughters of blue-collar workers, some were alcoholics, and many were war veterans. That school had the better basketball and football teams. We were better in track & field and wrestling teams.

I felt frightened entering Senior High School. I felt inferior. I had to prove something to those kids of money and to myself. From years of being told I was a "no good, dirty, son-of-a-bitch" by my alcoholic father and receiving no support from my alcoholic mother, I was not well prepared for appropriate social interaction with others. What I did have was my speed in track, which gave me some recognition. Regardless, I had low self-esteem and felt inferior to other kids.

Veronica said it best. "We were never the same after we left Jeff."

David Nelson Nelson

"Life Lessons Learned"

During my years at Jefferson Junior High School, I learned some valuable life lessons that I have carried with me to this day.

Laughter is good medicine

The laughter that all of us pals experienced was good for me. It helped to suppress my anxiety and depression. It afforded me the opportunity to live in a safe world – if only for a moment in time.

Pals are a link to inner peace

The pals I had back then are still with me today. We remain friends even to this day. It is because we care about one another.

Listen with your heart

As a child I could tell when others listened to me. The fact they listened meant they cared. Whether it was Rex squinting his eyes and peering into mine, Veronica on the phone paying attention, Mrs. Reid leaning forward in her chair, or when Mrs. Cierney stopped chewing on her thread to hear one of my tales, they all cared.

Green Jello can be good for the soul

Sometimes Lutherans can be such simple folk. That is a good thing. I like traditions.

You can tell a lot about people by the way they walk

From the window below in Mr. Grant's home I saw different kinds of walkers. The common thread was their past. They all had one, and I often wondered about that. I still wonder today when I meet people.

We all have dented pasts and yet we are all precious

Watching my pal, Tom burn and dent a new model car that he created and cherished was a good thing for me to see. I am full of dents and that is what makes me special.

"It's better to get your ass kicked once than picked on for an eternity"
Bryan Mihalakis

When I see a problem or a challenge I confront it head on and attack. One time in my life adversity "kicked my ass", but for the most part I succeeded – including that twenty-mile hike in Boy Scouts. Thanks, Richard.

Words can punish or harm more than anything else

I learned this from Mrs. Reid when I stole that car. I learned that from my mother my entire life.

"Some children experience their childhood and then spend the rest of their lives trying to get over it."
Unknown

Growing up in a dysfunctional home and a rotted neighborhood has a tendency to create an individual who learns to live by their wits. Due to their anxiety, they are always looking for danger in their environment and how to manipulate things for their own protection. However, after looking and studying my past I now embrace it. I have moved forward.

A yarn or a story can be repeated the same way more than once. A lie cannot.

I am a storyteller and a humorist. I am also known as the "Biggest Liar in East Tennessee" when I perform my "Cowboy Comedy

David Nelson Nelson

Show." Mrs. Cierney, Mrs. Johnson and I all have T-times for golf at twelve noon. Anyone want to join us?

Section III

Dubuque Senior High School

David Nelson Nelson

"Smoking"

I was allowed to smoke at home by the time I reached age fourteen. During high school, smoking was a part of my everyday life. It made me feel tough. It made me stand out and feel special. Smoking was glamorous. The tobacco companies convinced me and many others of the untruth that we swallowed as truth. I walked the line between trying to emulate my friend Rex who followed all the rules and being one of the bad boys on campus.

Tom was also allowed to smoke at home the same time as me. I supposed it was because our parents were tired of us stealing cigarettes from them. My dad continued to beat me and I continued to find reasons not to go home each night after school. Each summer, there were weeks on end when I stayed at Tom's home and was never questioned by my parents as to my absence. His folks knew of my situation and gladly offered refuge. In fact, Tom's dad used to joke that he was going to use me as a deduction on his taxes. Many of us continued to despise the Establishment. Smoking bonded some of us together. Tom, Jim, Kosta, and I all smoked. Rex and Veronica did not. Yet, despite the different paths we all took in high school, all of us remained pals.

Rex and Veronica were in an upper level college preparatory track in school. Kosta and I were in a general college prep level. Jim was in a different sort of situation. He was in the general studies level. He had Catholic friends who attended the other high school in town who were required to attend summer school all through high school because they'd failed to meet the required standards. Apparently, Jim was bored and as a result registered for the same classes with his Catholic friends each summer. I think I would rather have broken pop bottles than to attend summer school.

By the time Jim was a senior at our school, he had enough credits to graduate by the end of the first semester. He was assigned to the athletic director and asked to file papers all semester. Only Jim would do such a thing. Tom, meanwhile, had quit school and was working in the community. He initially worked at a fast food restaurant. After that job, he worked at an optical store grinding lenses. Eventually his love of auto mechanics took him to a job driving heavy equipment and repairing engines.

Across the street from our school was Johnnie's Café. The five stools perched at the counter sat atop a linoleum floor. Off to one side were three booths and four small tables. When the lunch bell rang Johnnie's filled like a diner in New York City with elbow-to-elbow standing room only. This was a place where students were allowed to go for lunch and buy a cherry Coke and hamburger among other items. Students were allowed to smoke out front. At times the front of the store looked like a bomb went off because so many kids were smoking. The smoke encircled their heads like wreaths. For me, and a couple others who were involved in sports, we had to sneak around back and light up because coaches would peek out the windows trying to spot athletes.

Three of us sprinters on the track team never played football. The football season occurred the same time as cross-country. The track coach made us participate with the cross-country team in the fall. This was a ridiculous sport in my opinion. Those people who run long distance must have a screw loose. Why would anyone want to run miles on end? I didn't get it. If there's gas in the truck, then why run? We practiced at Bunker Hill Golf Course. Well, the other members of the team practiced. The three of us who were sprinters had our own version of practice. We each hid three cigarettes in our jock straps along with a pack of matches. We waddled stiff-legged the three blocks to the course and found an elevated green to lie against. There we were lying on our backs and smoking while the other kids were running four and five miles.

In the spring, at the Drake Relays, the same three of us sprinters found a vacant locker room. We pushed a row of lockers away from the wall, opened a window, and leaned out puffing away on our cigarettes. We watched the mass of people below entering to watch one of America's largest track & field events. We heard, "First call, 440 Relay," announced over the speaker system. Flipping our cigarettes out the window after a final drag, we left and headed to the track. That was the day we set two records. The slowest kid on our team was the only one who did not smoke. Sometime during my tenure as a sprinter one of the assistant coaches tattled on me to the head coach. He reported that I smoked. The head coach said, "Find out what brand and pass them to the other kids." I should have sent that assistant coach to my dad for tattling.

There was a committee at Senior High School called the Grounds Committee. It was comprised of students who had free rein to walk the halls and check locker rooms for students either skipping class or misbehaving in some way. The committee was reserved for students with good behavior and decent grades. We were all given round, blue badges to wear. For some reason, the committee picked my friend and me to be on this committee. He was one of the smokers with me on the track team. Yep, you've probably figured out what we did. There were many hiding places in the school that was built in 1858. We knew all of them. We smoked in the gym behind the press box while lying on the floor hiding. We smoked in an old locker room that was no longer used. We smoked behind the storage shed near the football team. We smoked everywhere. We had authority and felt important. One day I skipped my Grounds Committee duties and decided to take an early lunch.

Rex plopped his books down at our lunch table and joined Jim and me. "So what trouble have you been in lately? I'm almost afraid to ask."

It had been several weeks since we last talked but always managed a wave in the busy hallway. Senior High had over 1,500 students in grades ten through twelve. There were a little over 500 in our sophomore class alone.

"Who, are you talking to me?" Jim smiled and tapped his index finger to his chest.

With a chuckle, Rex countered, "I want to hear from both of you nimrods. It seems like we never get to talk much anymore."

PALS: Part One

Jim used both hands to motion Rex and me to join him at the center of the table. We obliged and were excited to hear a good story. "OK, do you guys know what I mean by pennying-in a door?"

"No - what the heck are you talking about," Rex and I asked in unison.

"OK, don't tell anyone, well especially Kosta. I learned how to penny a door from my older brother Mike. What you do is take a stack of pennies, push in the top of a door and stick the stack between the door and the jam. Then you do the same thing in the lower part of the door. What happens is the shape of the door becomes an "S" and can't be opened. It's so funny to watch people try to get the door opened. That's why I was late for lunch today." Jim slapped his hand on the table, laughed and sat back upright, his proud chest bulging out like he was expecting somebody to pin a medal on him.

I tapped Jim's shoulder with the back of my open hand. "All right, how does this work again? Does it work on all doors? What does this have to do with you being late today?" Rex nodded in agreement.

In a loud whisper we heard him say, "Yeah it works on all doors but a wooden one is the best. I figured I'd try it on a metal locker door today. And it worked like you wouldn't believe. I stuck Kosta's locker door tighter than a drum. I put two stacks of pennies between the door and the metal frame. I stood across the hall pretending to read the announcement board while watching him from the corner of my eye. He opened his lock but tried and tried to open the door and it was stuck. He finally kicked the door and walked away. Boy, did he look pissed-off."

Rex and I laughed while hitting each other in the shoulder and Jim puffed up with a sense of arrogance about him. In the process I bumped Rex's German book onto the floor. We just kept laughing.

203

"Sorry about that, Rex. I didn't mean to knock your book on the floor."

Rex wiped his eyes with a handkerchief while bending down to pick up his book. "That's fine. I hate that class anyway. That teacher, Miss Reu is tough. Forget about it."

We breathed a huge sigh and just when things calmed down, Kosta sat down and slammed his milk carton on the table.

"Where's your lunch?" I asked knowing the answer.

"Son of a bitch! I can't get my locker open to get it," he said to anyone who would listen. "I tried that damn door three or four times. It wouldn't budge. I am so pissed off!"

None of us listened. We became hysterical, shoving each other, howling and about falling off our stools at the lunch table. I saw milk squirt out of Jim's nose. I saw students laughing two tables away because we were laughing. I saw Rex shove his German book to the floor so he had room to prop his head on his forearm. When his book hit the floor we laughed at that. We probably would have laughed at a fly on the table. Kosta, however, did not see anything funny. He was just mad as hell and stared out the window as if no one was there. He sucked in air thru his one nostril, his left leg was bouncing up and down as if he had Parkinson's disease and his tightened fist nearly squeezed the milk from the carton.

In the afternoon while patrolling the empty halls I noticed Jim prying the pinched pennies from Kosta's locker.

I was still grinning from lunch period a couple hours before. "Where did you get that letter opener?"

"I took it off Miss Cain's desk when she turned around. She thinks I'm in the bathroom." Jim laughed as the last of the pennies hit the floor.

Jim returned to class and I continued my patrol looking for another hiding place.

Kosta never did know what happened that day. So if you see him, don't say anything.

David Nelson Nelson

"Wareco"

Wanting to buy a car and then needing insurance, cigarette money, and spending money, I had no other choice. I had to find a job. My first regular job was at Wareco Gas Station on the two corners of Rhomberg and Lincoln Avenues. I lied about my age and began working at fifteen rather than the minimum age of sixteen. All three of my brothers worked at Wareco. It was an easy walking distance two blocks from home. The money was tight and too often I was short of cash. Tom was always there to loan me some cash until payday and I always paid him back. Holding down a job during my younger years trained me for what was to come. I have worked every day of my life until I retired.

Our dress code for work was a white shirt with the Wareco emblem on it, white, baggy pants and shoes of our choosing. The worst part was a white pointed paper cap we had to wear. All of us workers thought it looked ridiculous. When a patron drove in, all the workers had to run to the car and with a pre-arranged comment say, "Welcome to Wareco, how may we help you?"

If he or she asked for two dollars worth of gas, the employee responsible for washing the windows would have to yell with a smile, "Two dollars on regular."

The other workers checked the tire pressure and another checked the oil after popping the car's hood. The window washer cleaned all the car's windows and side mirrors. All of this was done with each and every car. When there was only one car at the pumps, there were four or five kids surrounding the car like a pit stop during a NASCAR race. My pants were too large for my tiny frame and were held up by a belt that required me to punch an extra hole into it. I was so short I could never reach the center of the windshield even standing on my tip toes like that first day I met Veronica. That familiar position was no problem because I had years of experience reaching up to kiss after a loss at ping-pong. I hated washing windows and still do to this day. I do like to play ping-pong, however.

That stupid, ridiculous paper cap always fell off on to the patron's hood. One time a regular customer about nineteen years old came in for gas. I was trying to wash his windshield and my cap fell off. He turned on his wipers and they snagged my cap crumpling it into a mangled mess. "Hey, how do like that Shorty?"

"Oh, I don't care."

And I didn't care because he actually did me a favor. However, each time he returned and if I was checking tires, I always let air out of the right rear tire. "Shorty" my ass.

In 1964, public phone booths were located every few blocks. The cost to make a call was a dime. The phones were dial, rotary types where the caller had to place one finger in a slot and dial the number. They were black in color and had a round, projected coin return button in the upper right.

"Hey, Dave, come here," John Ansel said to me one day. "I'll show you something pretty neat."

John was a seventeen-year old worker at Wareco who attended Senior High and also lived in the neighborhood. He was much more experienced and since I enjoyed learning from the old guys at work, I joined him. We walked to the corner of the station next to the sidewalk. There sat a pay phone inside a booth.

"OK," he said as he took a nickel out of his pocket. "Watch this. It's all in the timing."

He inserted the coin into the slot and immediately hit the coin return with the base of his thumb. The nickel came back out and wow! We had a dial tone and could make a call for free. What a neat trick, I thought.

And for days when things were slow at work and the boss left for the night, I would practice over and over with the phone until I was better than any other kid who worked there. I could make a call from anywhere for nothing. I called grocery stores asking if they had Sir Walter Raleigh (tobacco) in a can and when told affirmative, I'd tell them to let him out. I would call different bars over and over looking for a fictional character that the bartender would then yell out asking for whatever name I said. I would order pizzas for people from Luigi's Pizza Palace. Sometimes I would just call anybody in the phone book and burp.

Naturally I called Veronica. I never told her what I did as she would just give me another lecture about what was right and what was wrong. I knew the difference. It was a few years later the phone company changed the coin return system to a lever rather than a button style. That ended my free phone usage. I like to think I had a part in changing America's communication industry.

"Looking Good"

I was tired of competing against the sons of dentists, lawyers and doctors with my shabbiness and general attire. I could not afford new glasses in the tenth grade. The tiny screw that held the frame together fell out so I replaced it with a safety pin. The black frames had specks of plastic chipped off. One night in Tom's basement he painted my frames a shiny black color reserved only for the finest model cars. I looked like the rock star, Buddy Holly (except for the safety pin).

I used either duct tape or black electrician's tape to wrap around my shoe for several weeks when the sole came loose. The only thing worse than a flopping shoe sole is a wobbly wheel on a grocery cart. Both can be humiliating. My socks had holes in the heels, my pants lacked a belt loop, and I probably had a hole in my jock strap for all I remember. But my glasses made a fashion statement.

J.C. Penny Company was located on Main Street in downtown Dubuque. The trusting staff worked in more than one department, and like many stores, they needed more employees. I had a foolproof plan to improve my look. Just like at Spahn and Rose Lumber Company when we stole the plank of wood and like the time I stole the bicycle from Municipal Pool, I walked into J.C. Penny like I owned the place. I knew my size and went right to the round racks of slacks. I picked three pair and went to the dressing room. That day I had worn my older brother's pants so I would have ample room for another pair. I thought for a moment about wearing my baggy Wareco pants, but even thieves have a line they won't cross. I slid a pair of cotton slacks on and covered them with my brother's pants. I pulled my shirt outside to help cover the bulk at the waist.

I put the other two pair back on the shelf and in a matter of minutes was walking north up Main Street towards Betty Jane Candy Store. Tomorrow I would look good, I thought. It was some years later the clothing industry of America developed a system where they would place magnetic identifiers on all their clothing to prevent stealing. I like to think I had a part in changing America's clothing industry - just like I did with the beverage, auto, communication, and cigarette industries. I was just doing my part.

"Fill It Up"

During my senior year in high school, I don't believe I paid for gas more than a few times. I studied, planned and cased my marks during the day for what I referred to as night time fill ups. I kept two five-gallon gas cans in the trunk of my car at all times. Also in the trunk was a green, soft hose that measured eight feet long. I'd cut the metal connector from the end to slide into the gas tanks of cars without catching on something. During the darkness I parked behind a car and snuck up to the side where the gas cap was located. In less than 30 seconds I sucked the hose until the fluid began running and I inserted the other end into my five-gallon can. I then drove away at least one mile and repeated the process with another car. Habit gave way to reason when I thought for a minute about checking the oil and washing the windshield.

While one can was filling, the other was nearing completion. It was a regular self-service operation. I drove back to the first car, and in less than a minute I emptied the five gallons into my car, set the empty can into the trunk and drove back to get my second can. It was a good process but not great because it was time-consuming. Another problem with siphoning gas was that sometimes I would get a mouthful and by the end of the night my lips were irritated and turned white in color. I told Tom about my siphoning and one night he asked if he could go with me.

"I don't know. It can get pretty scary and you really have to have your wits about you," I said, feeling he needed to know the truth. "You'll need to pay attention about everything and wait sometimes a long time in the dark to be certain nobody is around."

"I can do it. I think it might be fun to help you. I have never siphoned before but I know I can do it. C'mon, let me go with you."

Against my better judgment, I took him out for a nighttime fill up. Also against my better judgment we went into a different neighborhood. I don't know why I did that, but it proved fatal. We parked on a side street near Loras College far from my familiar terrain in the North End. It seemed a car or house light would illuminate the street on a frequent basis.

Tom pushed his glasses up further onto his nose and flicked his cigarette out the open window. "How long do we just sit here?"

"Until things quiet down. This seems like a busy neighborhood."

I leaned into the steering wheel and looked in all directions. "All right, let's do it a different way this time. We'll get that car across the street where those hedges are real high and far from that streetlight. So, we need to drive up onto the other street behind this one. We'll park and sneak down that hill between those two houses. I'll get it going and then we run back to the car, give it a few minutes and come back and get our stash. We'll have to move quickly to empty the can into my car."

Moments later we quietly pushed our doors closed so as not to make a sound. I unlocked the trunk with my key and gave the metal can to Tom. "OK let's go down the hill," I whispered.

He nodded in agreement and we walked a fast pace between two houses. We were almost to the flat part of the yard when a backdoor light came on. Tom panicked, turned and ran as the door opened. He took off like a deer with the metal can clanging against his leg. In the darkness he did not see the clothesline and it caught him in the throat and flipped him to the ground.

He released his grip on the handle as he grasped his larynx in pain. Meanwhile the empty can rolled down the hill as more porch lights lit up throughout the neighborhood. A car stopped in the middle of the street and the fella driving got out to see what was happening.

"Hey, what are youse kids doing in our yard? Get out of here! Fred, there's some kids doing something out back," the lady yelled while standing in the open doorway.

I started into action. "Jeez, get up! Get out of here now you idiot. We're in deep shit," I yelled to Tom.

Adrenalin replaced his pain and again he was off in a sprint up the hill and we were peeling off in my car like we were racing at the Talladega Speedway. Two blocks away I saw the blue cop lights behind us. The cop was parked and probably taking information from the neighbors. Clutching the wheel I quickly turned down an alley, the car slid on the loose gravel when I slammed on the brakes and immediately flicked off the car lights. I ran to the trunk and set the remaining five-gallon can next to a garbage can. I threw the green hose over a four foot high picket fence, slammed the trunk and off we went. With evidence gone, we felt safe and eventually relaxed a bit.

Tom rubbed his throat and peered into the side mirror. "You know, if they spotted our car we had better hide somewhere."

"Yeah, good idea. I know just the place."

In less than ten minutes I pulled into the graveled, two-tiered parking lot at Senior High. There was some function going on and the lot was nearly full of cars but we found a place to park between two of them on the lower level. We sat for what seemed like hours reviewing what went wrong.

"Sorry I screwed up," Tom apologized. "I didn't even see that clothesline. Jeez, I hope the Old Man doesn't see anything on my neck."

"Just tell him it's a hickey from some Catholic girl sucking on your throat while you were trying to commit a major sin. It's not your fault. I have to come up with a better system anyway. Something will hit me."

And indeed a few minutes later something did hit me. "Holy crap."

Tom lunged to the floorboard trying to hide. "What is it? Cops?"

"No, relax," I laughed.

"Jeez, you scared the crap out of me."

I wanted to stretch out the intrigue and increase the drama. "OK, look behind us and tell me what you see."

Tom looked behind him and to both sides. "Cars in a parking lot. What else is there to see?"

"See how we're parked down here on this lower level with those cars above us? If I get a long hose and shove it into a tank of one of those cars up there and put the other end into my car I can just sit here and fill up. This is ingenious! All I have to do is come back here when there are night functions like now and find a car parked backwards with its rear end toward the downhill side of the lot." I knew I was rambling, but I didn't care. It was too good to pass up.

"God, you are nuts. But you know what? It will work as long as nobody sees you."

And so it was I attended the PTA meetings, the drama club events, and the musical programs from then on at Senior High School. However, I was in the parking lot (and didn't see a lot.)

"Bowling"

The Riverside Bowling Alley sat about a block away from the Municipal Swimming Pool. The parking lot backed up to the Mississippi River. Once a year, the city of Dubuque was attacked by fish flies – also known as mayflies. They hatched from eggs deposited into the bottom sediment of the river. They spend up to three years as nymphs under the water. When temperature conditions are right they ascend to the surface, dry their wings and swarm in flight.

These creatures emerge by the hundreds of thousands to mate for a single twenty-four hour period. They have no mouth and no digestive system. Their sole purpose is to mate, lay eggs, become food for fish, frogs and other marine life and then die. The female lays up to 8,000 eggs in the river. During the night they were attracted to any kind of outdoor lights. It was not unusual to see cars that were parked under a streetlight to be covered like snow in a blizzard. Only these creatures were alive. They stunk like rotted fish and crunched when we stepped on their wings and bodies. The city used street cleaners to scrape the streets clean of the crusty pests.

I parked my car by the side door of the bowling alley. All the outdoor lights were off and the lot was in total darkness because of the fish flies.

"Come on, guys. Let's get a pop or something and try to blend in," I said as we got out of my car.

Randy let out a loud belch that echoed off the cars in the parking lot. "What do you want us to do?"

Randy Kretchmeyer was Jim's neighbor who was a Catholic and who attended Wahlert High School. He was a little slow with common sense, but a nice kid.

"Just look like you're watching someone bowl while I get the one I want," I told him.

Jim pulled change from his pocket and hit me on the shoulder. "Dave, I've done some exciting things in my life, but this could be the best."

Minutes later we were drinking Pepsi out of the five ounce glasses we ordered at the bar. There was more ice than pop. The others were watching a game on lane seventeen. I set my glass of ice down, picked up a black twelve pounder from the rack near the door and stuck the ball under my T-Shirt. All of us headed out the door toward my car. I had stolen a bowling ball and was bursting with pride as I plopped it on the front seat between Tom and me. And then I started the car. The crunching of the fish flies could not be heard over the four of us laughing. We sped away down Kerper Boulevard.

Off we went to my pre-determined spot. It was perfect as I studied the location every time I came down the steep 8th Street hill towards the *Telegraph Herald Newspaper* and downtown Dubuque. The street leveled off by Roshek's Department Store where years earlier I had stolen the necklace for that girl at Christmas. I didn't even remember her name anymore.

We drove up 9th Street and parked my car in the island joining 8th and 9th together. For months I studied curve balls, hooks and spot-throwing bowling balls. I even broke down and spent money that I stole from my sister's purse so I could try different maneuvers at the bowling alley. With all that under my belt, I was ready. I put the car in park, jumped out with Tom and Jim. I looked back and saw Randy was in the back seat crunching on ice from a glass.

"What the hell are you doing," I asked him. "Did you steal that glass from Riverside?"

"Yeah, if you guys can steal a bowling ball I can steal a glass full of ice," he said between crunches.

I ignored him and turned my attention to better things. "All right, watch this. I have it planned perfectly. I am about to throw a hook where the ball will curve left down the hill past those parked cars and speed up to fifty miles per hour as it hits something like *KDTH Radio Station* or anything else in the way. I planned this for months." I looked around to see if anyone was impressed. "Are you ready?"

"Hurry up before the cops come," Randy said smashing his glass near my back right tire.

I straightened my knees, my left leg in front of my right, my fingers placed perfectly in the holes. My left hand helped cradle the ball like world champion bowler Don Carter and my torso was bent to a twenty-degree angle. I took the mandatory three steps and a slide like I was taught in physical education at Jeff. I released my left arm, extended my right arm to hip level and with perfect timing, threw the ball as I rolled my hand over and palm down. It was a perfect curve to the left - for about ten feet. It hit a rock, veered right and after hitting an even larger rock was air borne! Oh crap, I thought.

In less than fifteen seconds, it was probably going the fifty miles per hour I had projected. Only it was in the air. In the air! When car windows break they do so into neat little squares. The only problem is they make an exploding sound. Yep, the ball went right through the back window of a 1957 Ford Fairlane parked at the curb, shot out its front window and as a curtain call, smashed the trunk of a 1955 Chevy parked in front of the Ford.

Even though all lights were off due to the fish flies, at the sound of breaking glass, the entire area immediately lit up with front porch lights. We piled into my car. I hit the gas and laid rubber as we peeled away. We were all laughing and hitting each other with crazed delight. All my calculations had been in error.

I raced my car up 8th Street. Tom yelled to me, "Hey, let's go fill your car up with gas."

David Nelson Nelson

"Henry Stole My Rabbits"

It was a typical hot and humid, night in July of 1966. Jim, Kosta, Tom and I were riding around in Tom's car. We asked Rex to come along, but he was too tired from water skiing all day. We called it puttin' the gut, where we drove up and down Main Street several times. Boredom once again overcame us. Boredom can be a good thing under the right circumstances. Boredom can lead to new adventures, and this night was no different.

"Hey, Tom I saw a car just like yours today," I said in a teasing manner.

"No way. There's only one of these cars in all of Dubuque. I put a lot of custom accessories on this baby," he said proudly. "It's a 1962 Chevy Chevelle with baby moon hub caps, a 327 engine with V-8."

I knew nothing about cars except how to put the gas in and clean the windows. "So it has four on the floor and two in the back seat?"

Everyone laughed and Kosta called me a dip shit.

"I like the color. What do you call this?"

Tom sat up straighter behind the wheel and flicked his cigarette out the window. "Baby Blue."

"Yep, it was just like your car," I said as he punched the gas and shifted gears. There was no reaction from my tease. He knew I was toying with him.

From the corner of my eye I saw Kosta wipe his forehead with his hand. "Jeez, this heat is killing me. What time is it?" He didn't wait for an answer. "Hey, I have an idea."

I turned toward the back seat where Jim and Kosta were sitting. "It's nine thirty. Why? What's your idea?"

"Pull over there by that little store so I can fill you in."

Tom put the car in park and turned off the headlights. "OK, what's up?"

"There's this crazy ole drunk guy who hangs out at the White House Tap back there. Ya know, those steps that go up to Angela Street from down here? They come out behind Loras College? Well, he gets drunk about every night and walks home up all those steps. We can have some fun harassing him."

Jim laughed out loud and Tom and I just looked at each other. "Is his name Henry? If it is, I heard about this from my brother Mike," Jim said.

"You got it."

"Why, what's the point? What are we going to do?" I asked.

"Like I said, he's crazy and if we yell, "Henry stole my rabbits," he gets real pissed off and will chase us. Now this guy is a fast runner, drunk or sober. Come on. It'll be fun. A bunch of us did it to him last year and it was a riot."

Tom scratched his head. "So what's the deal with stealing rabbits?"

"I don't know. Apparently some neighbors accused him of stealing their rabbits and the guy got in a fistfight or something. All I know is that it works and sets him off pretty good."

I pointed to the bar behind us. "So what do we do? Just sit here all night? We don't know if he's even in that bar."

Kosta pushed against the front seat. "Let me out. I'll go buy some smokes and see if he's there. He always wears a green ball cap sideways and is a little wiry fella."

I opened my door and pulled the seat forward so Kosta could get out. He walked towards the bar while I leaned against the open door on the sidewalk waiting for him to return.

A couple minutes later he came running down the street clapping his hands in excitement. "We're in luck. He's paying the tab. Come on, let's go! Hurry, Tom, you drive up the hill and we can get ready for him. We can park the car at the far end of the street and run down towards him."

Tom shook his head as he shifted gears. "Oh no. Not me. I'll be in the car ready to drive away as soon as you morons come back. I don't want to get in trouble."

A couple minutes later Tom was behind the wheel of his parked car while Kosta, Jim and I trotted down the street passing parked cars and occasional streetlights. Like everywhere else in the North End, the houses were a few feet from one another with postage size yards in front and larger, narrow yards in back filled with clotheslines. It was quiet for such a hot summer night and odd that nobody was sitting on front porches. Good for us, bad for Henry.

We slowed our pace and came to a stop when Jim pointed and whispered, "Holy crap. There he is already. See him down there by that third street light?"

Henry didn't stagger and didn't appear drunk. In the stillness I did hear him talking to himself and at times even yelled like he was having an argument with an invisible someone.

"Hey, Henry you dink! Henry, you twit! Why did you steal my rabbits?" Kosta yelled at the top of his lungs and scared me at first.

Henry stopped dead in his tracks and ended the argument he was having with himself. In a shrill voice, he screamed back at us, "Shut up. Shut up you sons-a-bitches."

In unison we all cackled and yelled even louder, "Henry stole my rabbits. Henry stole my rabbits."

This time there was no response from Henry. We heard nothing. We saw nothing. He was gone from the streetlight and gone from the street. We knelt down looking under cars and sprang to the sidewalk to check for his location. There was nothing.

Jim was bouncing up and down in the street like a sprinter getting ready for a race. "Get ready, Dave. He'll be coming from somewhere. So let's see some of your lightning speed."

The adrenalin filled me as my muscles tightened and I assumed the standing start position, when out of nowhere I heard footsteps coming from the dark at bullet speed. Oh shit I thought as I took off. I saw Tom's brake lights ahead and heard him start the Chevelle. Closer and closer the leather soles of Henry's shoes were behind me. I thought for a moment I felt his hand swipe my back just like I experienced with Mr. Grant years before. I increased my speed leaving him far behind.

I hadn't realized it, but Kosta and Jim had taken off running long before I did. They were in Tom's car and were yelling for me to hurry.

"Oh, Jeez. You crazy assholes!" Tom yelled as I piled into the car and we sped away. The four of us laughed and talked at the same time and were filled with excitement. I looked in the outside rear view mirror and saw Henry beneath a streetlight giving us the bird with both long fingers.

"Well I know what we are doing tomorrow night," I said, "Boy, that was fun. What a rush."

David Nelson Nelson

Jim leaned forward from the back seat and squeezed both of Tom's shoulders. "Tom, are you up for it?"

"Yeah, but I'm not leaving the car. I'll be the getaway driver again. You Butt Wipes are nuts."

"Henry: Part II"

It was ten P.M. when Kosta returned to the waiting car. "Oh nuts. He's not in the bar."

Tom was focused on blowing smoke rings against his rear view mirror and stopped for a second. "What are we going to do? Just ride around and come back later?"

Jim looked at me while Kosta was joining him in the back seat. "No, I have a better idea. Let's go to his house, stand outside and yell. If he's in there he sure as hell will come out on the run. I'll show you where he lives. His house is the oldest on the block. It's back several feet between two other houses. It's wooden siding that hasn't been painted in decades and is surrounded by real high shrubs."

Tom turned the corner and drove up the hill, made a right turn and turned again on Angela Street. He backed up, turned around and kept the engine running while Jim and Kosta climbed out of the back seat and I climbed out of the front.

My shirt was soaked from the humidity. The area seemed deserted as a ghost town except for the quiet hum of an occasional window air conditioner. In fact, there was total darkness between each streetlight. There was not a porch light lit on the entire block.

Tom leaned forward and looked out the passenger side window. "Tonight I'll be pointed up the hill by the football field. I want to make sure nobody can see my plates and I will have a better view of you three morons when he starts chasing you up the street."

With a near skip in our steps we talked about the quickly laid plan. Kosta stopped us in the shadow of a streetlight. "OK, we'll walk up to the front of his house and, trust me, we've done this before. If he's home, we won't be able to tell because he sits in the dark and either talks to himself or watches TV."

I listened intently as I wiped sweat from my face and head with my shirt. "Oh, Jeez this is going to be fun."

Three minutes later we were in Henry's tiny, pitch-black front yard. The numerous fireflies offered the only light. It was total darkness and we felt an eerie calm among the high shrubs. I heard the faint rumble of Tom's muffler off in the distance. We were about ten feet from the wooden structure and began yelling in unison.

"Henry stole my rabbits. Henry stole my rabbits. Henry..."

Ka-boom! I saw the flames from the shotgun just a millisecond before I heard the blast. In an instant I thought I saw a wiry little fella with a ball cap sideways on his head as he fired the weapon. Henry was standing with his back to the house behind the bushes. Adrenaline overtook me and I was off in a sprint like the 100-yard dash at the Drake Relays.

Once again, porch lights lit up the street and dogs started barking nearby and even below on West Locust Street. Doors were thrown open and I heard the loud muffler from Tom's car as he laid rubber leaving the scene a block away.

In his high pitched voice I heard Henry behind me scream, "You sons-a-bitches! You had better run or next time I will kill all of you little dirt bags."

I hurdled the two-foot high limestone wall that separated Henry's house from the Koernshield's home and ducked under the clothesline. I had a perfect view and it was like a nighttime track meet as every outdoor light was illuminated.

Mrs. Koernshield came out the back. She was wearing a blue housecoat and her hair was in curlers ready for church tomorrow at St. Peter Lutheran Church. I was amazed at how every detail was caught with all my senses during a state of fright. I watched her set her horned-rim glasses perfectly on her nose. I smelled either the scent of perfume or Ivory soap from her recent shower. I remembered hearing the howl of a beagle at least two blocks away when I saw Mrs. Koernshield look me in the eyes just before I sprinted around the corner and headed for the street and to the freedom of Tom's car.

"Dave," she said. "What happened? What's going on? What are you doing in my yard," she asked as I shot around the corner of her house and out onto the street.

Oh nuts, I thought. She had seen me and tomorrow at church I would get the third degree.

The oak, maple, and elm trees were lit with a blue flashing light as a cop car was screaming up Loras and headed our way. I saw Tom's car blinker as he turned to the right and drove away.

Under the street lights the three of us stopped to catch our breath and make another plan. This was not my style as I always thought and analyzed every caper. I was out of my element and out of control.

"Aw shit. Here he comes," I said as the cop turned off his siren but kept the blue lights on and headed toward us. "Just play dumb. Pretend like we heard the shot and saw nothing other than three kids running the other direction down the street."

The cop seemed excited when he left his car. "Hey youse guys hold it right there now! Do not move. Do youse understand me?"

Jim hit me in the ribs with his elbow. "Look at that cop. It's Degnan who took us in for breaking bottles."

"Aw crap. Maybe he won't remember us or recognize us here in the dark."

Kosta took the lead. "Jeez, what is going on, officer? We walked up here from West Locust and heard a gunshot or a cherry bomb. All of a sudden three kids ran right past us headed for the steps and toward West Locust."

David Nelson Nelson

"What are youse three doing? So it wasn't youse guys picking on that old man?"

"What old man?" I asked and continued. "No, we were headed up to McDonald's on University Avenue."

"What are your names? Let me see some identification? Nelson? Do you run track at Senior?"

"Yes, officer. It's nice of you to recognize me."

"Do you know my nephew, Jamie Degnan? He ran the half mile and is a senior next year?"

"Jamie? Why sure what a nice guy. He has a lot of great potential."

In reality I didn't know that kid from Adam and Eve but tried my best to get him to let us go. There we were standing in a semi-circle talking track and I just wanted to get the hell out of there as neighbors were coming up the street like a lynch mob. All of a sudden from out of the darkness, Tom came among us. "Holy shit! Get the hell out of here. Where did that cop go?"

It was then I realized Tom must have lost his mind. He did not see the cop standing right there next to us. It was then I figured Tom had inhaled too much of the burning plastic from his melted model cars over the years. It was then I knew we were in deep trouble.

A fat guy with a beer belly was leading the hoard of neighbors toward us. "That's the guys, officer. That's the punks who harassed Mr. Klinkiemeyer and made him shoot his gun off."

The cop lit up our faces with his powerful flashlight. "Ya know something? One thing I absolutely detest is a liar. And youse three boys are liars. Get into the back seat of my car right now." He shined his light on Tom. "And who are you?"

Officer Degnan turned his attention to the crowd. "How many were there? Did anybody see?"

The beer-bellied boozer pointed a finger at Tom. "Naw, he wasn't with the other three. I didn't see him at all. But those are the guys sure enough. I was sitting in the dark on my porch across the street having a Star Beer. I saw those three guys under the streetlight."

"Was anybody else around then?" Officer Degnan asked the fella.

"Naw, just me. The old lady was doing dishes in the zink and I was outside by myself."

The cop looked at Tom. "OK, you're free to go and I never want to see you in this neighborhood again. Do you understand?"

I looked out the back window of the squad car and saw Tom trotting up the street to where he parked his car. During the ride to the police station, Jim whispered to me that Officer Degnan did not remember us. What a relief!

It was about midnight when I got home that night. The cops carded us again and let us go. They must have stopped calling parents when kids were carded. I walked home and interrupted a euchre game in the kitchen. I told Ma, Dad, Richard and a friend of Richard's that night what happened. That was the first time my dad actually thought my pranks were funny. There was no beating only everyone listening to my great story and laughing. I felt like I was entertaining a crowd of thousands while performing my storytelling. Mrs. Cierney and Mrs. Johnson would have been proud of my oratory skills.

David Nelson Nelson

"The Edsel"

She was an ugly green. The showroom shine was replaced by a dull hue like an old weathered woman without makeup. There was a six-inch hole in the floorboard next to my left foot. The rusty doors squeaked each time they were opened or closed. The windshield wipers were vacuum pumped. When the gas pedal was depressed, the wipers would change speed to a rapid slapping across the glass barrier and then go into a pattern of slow motion when the gas pedal was not used. The seats were torn and tattered. The clock did not work. The door to the glove compartment would fall open each time the car hit a bump or pothole. I propped it closed with a folded-over package of matches.

I really liked her. She was my first car, a 1960 Ford Edsel, named after one of Henry Ford's sons. The Media called the Edsel all kinds of names. One reporter wrote, "It's like an Oldsmobile sucking a lemon; Or a Pontiac pushing a toilet seat."

I saved enough money working at Wareco Gas Station during the eleventh grade to make the $200 purchase. The first thing I did was to get some classy seat covers from the Fingerhut Corporation. They were plastic and had little bumps all over them. I enjoyed making out with my girlfriend in the front seat on those Fingerhut seat covers. The only problem was that they were slippery and when I got too fresh, she would give me a shove and off I slid to the floor and the old familiar transmission hump. I was a quick learner and little for my age. I learned to wrap my left leg through the steering wheel and latch on like a leach. Nothing or nobody could pry me loose then. Although there was one time my leach-latching didn't work. That darn glove box door popped open for no reason and bonged me on the back of my head. There I was hooked to the steering with my foot, bleeding from my head and lying on the floor. I was lucky I didn't pull a muscle or something even worse.

Unfortunately, there was nothing I could do about the lost sheen no matter how many times I applied wax. To dress her up so I could take her out, I put a four-inch wide, black racing stripe

PALS: Part One

starting from the trunk, over the top and across the hood. It was black and gained attention by just about everyone when I passed by. They pointed, laughed and hit one another. But that was ok, I liked to make people laugh and I still do.

Gaining attention was important to me. On the inside, I suffered terrible bouts of depression and anxiety, especially at home. Living at Tom's house all summer long helped immensely and being there after school on weeknights also helped. But I was sad and I was lonely. Now that I had a car I had freedom and in my mind, that meant control. I was important. I accepted the hole in the floor and quickly learned to lift my left leg whenever I drove through standing water. At night, however, if I was focused on some girl next to me, and didn't see the upcoming puddle, I would get soaked. To a sixteen year-old boy, that was embarrassing walking with her to her front door with a left pant leg soaked and a sloshing sound coming from my shoe. I sure am thankful I didn't have that car in the tenth grade when I walked around with a safety pin in my painted glasses and duct tape on my shoe. Sometimes in life timing is everything.

I had plans, three to be exact. First, my plan was to be the envy of my buddies. My plan was to have all the girls wanting to ride with me. But most of all, my plan was to make out at the Drive-In Theater on John Deere Road with any girl of my choosing. However, things did not work as planned. I didn't mind the laughter but I had to force my girlfriend to ride in my car. And somewhere between fantasy and reality, the darn thing fell apart. I never did make it to the drive-in theater with the old jalopy. She lasted about six months and blew the head. I received twenty-five dollars from Boyce Wrecking and Junkyard. I was ticked-off. I have no clue what 'blowing a head gasket' meant. I just put that in there to pretend to be cool. My next car was a 1958 Olds.

Truth be told, I had expected that to happen with my Edsel. But then I always seemed to expect the worst. I wonder if that came from always expecting some type of emotional or physical pain each time I opened the door to my house at 617 Lincoln Avenue. My mother would complain if she was hung with a new rope or

David Nelson Nelson

kicked in the butt with new boots. Nothing was ever good enough and she could suck the energy out of an F5 tornado without missing a beat. She complained to Dad constantly about us kids as a unit or on an individual basis. While she enjoyed snapping the backs of our legs and rear ends with a long lilac switch, I think her greatest joy was her famous last words. "Just wait until your dad gets home."

From the age of eight I lived in constant fear of waiting for Dad to get home. If I was one of the lucky ones not to be hit on any particular evening, I made certain I was quiet so as not to cross an unmarked line or break an untold rule. My dad's wrath could explode at any moment. I suspect living with Ma did that to him. He was probably just as miserable as us kids and tried to hide it with alcohol. However, things were not always terrible.

Dad sometimes had a good streak and a dry sense of humor. There were times when he was happy. Those times were when he was busy with his night and weekend job of operating "Nelson's T.V. Business" out of the house. He was self-taught from studying manuals. He knew every tube, capacitor, make and model of television on the market. I figure he dove into that business to avoid Ma and to help find money for a family of seven kids. Dad was intelligent.

Vacations when we were little were fun. I felt the air in the house begin to change months before we went on trips. I watched him separate copper from metal shavings he brought home first from Mazewood and then Celotex. These were the same buildings where he was a machinist. Mazewood was bought out by Celotex and Dad stayed on at his job. He would work for hours every night of every week (when he was not repairing a television) collecting the copper to sell for scrap. He may have sold to Kosta's father who operated a metal business. Why, heck he may have sold to Kosta himself. I sure hope not because Kosta would have put the screws to him being as he was shrewd even as a kid. Dad would spend hours on end reviewing the Rand's Atlas and planning our trips. He was so intelligent he never again looked at a map once we left the house. Each and every road was memorized. I watched him become a happy person just prior to and during our trips. That was nice.

PALS: Part One

He had a dream of seeing all forty-eight continental states in America. Us three older kids were the ones who went on the original trips while the younger two stayed with grandparents. The two youngest girls were not born yet. We drove in the family car that sometimes broke down from overheating. That is why there was always a gallon jug of water on the floorboard in the back. That is what Richard used for a pillow when curled up to sleep. I had the opposite side of the transmission hump while Margaret had the back seat. That is how we slept six out of seven nights traveling to a far destination in America. Rule number one was that we stayed in a motel only once during the week.

Rule number two was that us kids were never allowed to order our own food the rare times we stopped at a restaurant. My parents knew what was best. Rule number three was there was to be no fighting in the back seat and minimal talking.

Then, as now, I was really good at two things: studying human behavior and mathematics. I observed Dad from low in my vantage point on the right side of the backseat. When he started rubbing his head and messing up his hair even more than normal, I knew to be still. When he constantly shifted positions behind the wheel or held his head from driving fatigue I knew not to say a word. Richard and I would fight, poke, pinch, and say bad things to one another across Margaret's lap as she sat between us. Eventually Dad had enough and either my brother or I would have to lean toward the front seat so he could reach us. There would be the customary punch in the face or slap across the cheek. Those never hurt because he did not have a long enough lever arm to increase momentum and therefore power. (That was the only useable equation I learned in college physics). This event seemed to happen about every three hundred miles. I always asked Dad how far we would travel. Upon learning the answer I pulled a paper grocery sack from the stack wedged between the refrigerator and the counter. I took a pencil from the kitchen junk drawer and then went to work doing the math. I figured 300 miles per punch and divided that into the total miles. I figured how many punches the trip was worth. If I could get Richard involved a few more times than me, I would have a great vacation. Sometimes in life timing is everything.

231

Each time we vacationed, the three of us kids received five dollars spending money. Now *that* was exciting. During one vacation our first stop was the Mitchell Corn Palace in South Dakota. I was so proud of my wooden-handle, rubber-headed tomahawk that was made far away in China and cost $4.76. It was much better than Richard's headdress with plastic feathers and the tiny bow with one puny little arrow.

We stopped for gas somewhere near the famous Wall Drug Store. Richard jumped out of the back seat and with war on his mind put on his plastic bonnet, pulled back on the bow string to kill an empty potato chip bag, and "Pow!" the bow broke, broke into three pieces. He crawled into the back seat with crooked feathers half-cocked and began crying. Dad yelled to stop the crying or he would give him something to cry about. Margaret called him a baby. I simply slapped my tomahawk into my opened left palm like Miss Schroeder did with the *Wind-Whipper* and smiled. I figured if he kept crying I'd be good for another 300 miles without a punch or slap. Sometimes in life, as I keep saying, timing is everything.

I managed to protect my tomahawk all the way home. I placed it in the back window for protection. I had a secret plan and became excited when I thought of it. The day after we arrived home I found Richard's bonnet with bent plastic feathers sticking out from under his bed. "Hey, can I use this?"

"Heck no, get your own," he said.

I closed my right eye like a pirate and squeezed my brows toward each other. "Now where the heck am I going to find an Indian Headdress in Dubuque, Iowa, you nimrod?"

"I don't care. You're not using mine," he insisted as he sat on his bed trying to straighten the bent plastic feathers.

I shot him the bird and stomped across the room. "Go to hell!"

"I'm telling Dad," he said with a sense of pride.

I just blew some air out my closed lips and knew that would never happen. It was OK for Ma to tattle on us, but we would be beaten if we tattled on each other. I knew I was safe.

Tom and I were to meet at Audubon as we had discussed on the phone. I heard him bouncing his basketball walking up Lincoln while I was searching for a pigeon feather. I tied two shoestrings together that I had taken from my younger brother's good pair of shoes for church. I wrapped them around my head. After tying them behind my head I poked a pigeon feather in the back. I pretended to be a Sioux Brave. My name was "Coo-Hawk." Those words were a combination of the sound a pigeon makes and the last part of the word tomahawk. Pretty neat, huh? I spit on my fingers, rubbed them in the dirt and ran them across my face. That was my war paint.

Tom came toward me still bouncing his ball and said, "What the heck are you supposed to be with that pigeon feather in your hair? And what's on your face," he cackled as he fixed his glasses.

I straightened my right arm holding the tomahawk that was pointed at Tom. In a voice like Tonto on The Lone Ranger television show, I said, "How! I am Coo-Hawk. Pale Face wantum to get scalped?"

He shook his head left and then right and told me I looked more like Dumb-Ass.

Ignoring him, I returned to my regular voice. "Hey look at this. It's a tomahawk. It comes all the way from China. Let's go over by the fountain and see if we can kill a pigeon with it. I'll go first."

He dropped his basketball and we walked with intention to the single head bubbler. It was there that pigeons would gather before flying to the top of the school. And indeed, there was one walking around. Those birds are so dumb and easy to sneak up on it wasn't fair. But I didn't care. I was on the warpath. I was three feet away, raised my right arm, clung to the wooden handle, and let go with a war whoop! The wooden-handled, rubber-tipped tomahawk all the way from China exploded into a million pieces. I missed by a mile. It had hit the cement. Even the rubber head cracked – probably from a week's worth of heat in the car's back window. The pigeon kept walking in circles unfazed. Sometimes in life timing is everything.

Tom could have cared less one way or another. He picked up his ball and headed to the hoop. "Hey let's shoot some baskets."

I ripped the shoestrings from my head, dropped 'em to the ground and began playing basketball. I was still on a warpath, but one of a different nature. I had to beat him shooting hoops.

Other family vacations included fishing in lakes in Wisconsin and Minnesota. We swam in all five Great Lakes. Lake Superior seemed the coldest. I saw my first limousine in Hot Springs, Arkansas. We traveled by ferry from Ludington, Michigan to Milwaukee, Wisconsin. Crossing the Mackinac Bridge over to the island was great. There were no cars allowed on the island so we had to park in a lot and walk everywhere. I was out of allowance so I stole some fancy chocolate in a shop and ate it sitting on a rocker on the porch of the Grand Hotel. I was at peace.

On a trip through Yellowstone National Park, we came to a dead stop. There were hundreds of tourists running from their cars when I asked, "Dad, can we get out to see what's happening?"

"Hell, No! Those damn fools will probably be eaten by a bear," he growled.

No sooner had he said that when he yelled, "Roll up all the damn windows here comes some bears!"

And indeed they were. It was a mother and two cubs. They stopped at our car probably looking for food. My sister took pictures as fast as she could with her Browning Instamatic camera. The windows were still wet from the early morning dew and combined with the dust from the long trip, created a canvas for paw prints. Each bear stood on its hind legs and rested their paws on the passenger side windows. They snorted their breath against the glass and created steam on the windows. I touched the mother's paw with my hand through the glass. That was one of the most exciting things that happened to me as a kid!

We were not allowed to roll down either window on the passenger side of the car all the way home. As soon as we parked in front of 617 Lincoln Avenue, we three kids ran in different directions to tell everyone to come and look at the paw prints. Within fifteen minutes there must have been twenty-five children of all sizes shoving each other at the curb. They each wanted to have a peek at the bear prints. I was hot stuff and for the next two days kids bought me ice cream cones and pop from Huey's. That was the price I charged the boys to tell the entire and real story.

My story began like this: "There I was, off the road in some high grass. My dad let me leave the car to go take a pee. I even had a boner I had to pee so badly." The boys nodded, understanding what I meant. "The grass was a lot greener and higher on my side of the car. Ya know, that's where that saying comes from. Anyways, I was standing in grass up to my shoulders when I heard something. It sounded like a snort or a grunt of some kind. I saw steam coming up from a flat spot in the grass off to my left. I stopped trying to write my name in the grass with my pee. After I finished, I put my dick back into my pants and walked over to the mist. It was the biggest pile of poop I had ever seen. The stinky steam stunk more than fish flies. I started to walk back to our car. My dad was outside screaming for me to run. My brother, Richard was waving me on from the backseat window. You know I can run pretty fast – but I didn't know why I was supposed to run. Then I saw them. Three bears and one buffalo were all charging toward me. I took off in a sprint but it was no good. They were so close I saw flies on the buffalo's back and the big white teeth of the bears. I had to fight 'em off. I took off this red jacket – the very one I am holding now and began to wave it like one of those funny-looking guys in a bullfight. The buffalo crashed right through my coat and put a dent in the door. Dad already had it fixed, otherwise you could see it here. Anyways, the buffalo knocked itself out when in no time the big mama bear ran through my coat and came to a complete stop against the car window. She used her paws to keep from crashing through into the back seat. That's where we have these paw prints right here. Well she turned around and I kicked her right in the chest and she ran off gasping for air. The buffalo was asleep or something and just twitching on the ground. The baby bears saw what I did to their mother and knew not to mess with me. They ran off into the tall grass. I calmly opened the door and told Dad I was ready to go. That will be either a pop or an ice cream from Huey's. Pay-up."

I met my first Little Person at Timber Lakes Resort in Brainerd, Minnesota. He was about three feet high, drove a pickup truck and had more muscles than I did at age fourteen. He taught me how to put salt on leeches to make them fall off the skin. One day he took me riding in his beat-up truck and we spotted a moose standing alongside the road. He put the truck in neutral and we coasted up next to the moose. We sat there quietly for about five minutes watching the moose shake and knock flies off his hide while chewing grass like an Iowa cow. His breath could be seen when he exhaled and his big bulging eyes looked back at us. I enjoyed that moment of peace. I like Little People.

I saw my first African-American in Hot Springs, Arkansas. We pulled over in a commercial district for the night so Dad and Ma could sleep. Margaret was on the back seat and Richard and I were curled like cats on our floor mats. Ma and Dad slept sitting up. I was the first to wake. I saw an elderly African-American fella peeking into our cars windows. He was the first person of color I ever saw. What could I do but scream! Boy, did I scream. Everyone jumped to his senses and the little old guy went scrambling down the sidewalk. I was eight years old.

We went to The Great Smoky Mountain National Park. I saw Abraham Lincoln's log cabin in Illinois. I saw Mount Rushmore. I was at the Museum of Science and Industry in Chicago and saw the famous Arch in St. Louis. I was sprayed by Old Faithful and felt the hot springs in Wyoming.

PALS: Part One

As I reflect back, I remember those fine times traveling and how things reverted right back to the way they were the day after we returned home. It was sort of like my Edsel. At first I had the best time with it and was proud to have some freedom and attention paid to me. Then it fell apart and everything reverted right back to the way it was before. I was walking again. Sometimes in life, timing is everything. And that can be bad or good.

As with many events in life there is always a silver lining to any cloud. Tom was that silver lining for me. He had one of the neatest cars for any kid our age. It was a 1961, Chevy Bellaire, two-door sedan painted light blue with dark blue interior. It had a three-speed straight stick, six cylinder, and baby moon hubcaps. There were white wall tires and a 235 cc engine. The best part for Tom was the dome light. It was used many times in our adventures. I shall explain that later. The shift was on the column that allowed Tom to lean into the steering wheel with his left arm wrapped around the arc of the wheel. His right arm was on the shift and he would sit and rev the engine at every stoplight. He was master of his universe. If he drives like that now at his age, it's because he either has to fart or his back hurts.

I sat opposite him trying to make myself taller than my five-foot one-inch height. I tightened my butt cheeks and my anal sphincter muscle. It wasn't easy to push my ninety-three pounds toward the roof liner with my feet against the floorboard. I arched my back and pushed my spine into the seat. I gained an inch in vertical elongation. I wondered if that would work with another body part. Riding like that for hours has certain effects on the body. For years everyone thought I was a happy kid with a constant smile. I was simply in this locked position so I could see out the window. I was not smiling, I was straining. I still get this look today, but it's when I'm constipated.

That wasn't all I did. I propped my right arm on the window frame so as to push my biceps out flat and make me look powerful. If an opponent parked next to us at a light, I would first nod my head in recognition. Then without losing a stroke, I would flick my head in an attempt to straighten my blonde hair that hung across my left eye. I was somebody tough. Riding around with Tom sure beat the heck out of driving my Edsel.

We would putt the gut looking for chicks to possibly pick up and take for rides. We would spend many an evening at either the Point Drive-In restaurant on Rhomberg Avenue or the A&W on Dodge Street. We would order root beers and just sit in his car and watch the carhops or other girls milling about the area.

I knew I could always rely on Tom whenever I made plans with some girl. He never seemed to mind driving around town with my girlfriend and me. He also never seemed to mind driving when I convinced her to get in the back seat so we could make out. Many times I caught him looking in the rear-view mirror as I was going at it hot and heavy. I didn't care. Why should I? I was hormone-charged. We all were back in those days. I was so horny the crack of dawn wasn't safe. It was because of Tom that I had the good fortune to meet girls like Handy-Andy and Painted-Woman. There were times when he and his girlfriend were in the front and me with mine in the back. I did manage to make-out at the Drive-In Theater. Tom was my best pal back in high school and still is today.

There was one occasion that I must write about, as it is just too funny to pass up. Tom, his cousin, Jack, and I were cruising around town looking for girls. I had difficulty talking much that night as my butt cheeks were in constant contraction and I was more focused on my tightened arm hanging out the window. Then an idea hit me.

"Hey, let's go see if Sherry's home and see if she wants to go riding around."

Jack knocked the ash off his cigarette into the ashtray. "What, and we just sit in the front seat while you get some action in the back?"

"Aw, don't worry about it, Jack. We do this all the time. Sometimes I even get a pretty good show in the rear view mirror."

PALS: Part One

A short time later I was in the back with Sherry Smickelhoff and had my jacket over our laps. We had been French-kissing up a storm and I was ready to move on to bigger and better things. The sound of her unzipping my pants was heard in the front seat. Laughter abounded.

"What's so funny up there? What are youse two laughing at," Sherry asked.

Tom cocked his head up to look into the rear view mirror as he drove the darkened street on the way to Comisky Park. "Oh, nothing. It was just a joke we heard today."

I didn't care why they were laughing. I was on a mission and wanted satisfaction. I'm not certain if it was my jacket jumping in a rapid up and down motion that Tom saw in the mirror; or if it was my high pitched moan that caused the next great event.

On the corner of Jackson and East 23rd Streets he stopped at a stop sign. Now he did not just come to a complete stop like the driver's manual taught us. He came to a full stop, put the car in park, and turned on the dome light. He and Jack turned around from the front seat and all jacket movement came to a screeching halt. My Mister Howdy went into immediate shrinkage mode, as Sherry ripped her arm out from under my jacket and tried her best to play innocent.

"What the hell are you morons doing?" I asked with rapid breaths and in a high shrill voice, leftovers from Mister Howdy standing at attention seconds earlier.

"Nothing. We just wanted to see what was going on back there." Jack said as both he and Tom began laughing out loud.

It was no time at all before we dropped Sherry off at her house and I climbed into the front seat. For some reason, she and I never did go on a date again. As the three of us drove to the A&W, those two idiots would make high-pitched sounds of moaning and squealing. The event came to be known as the Jumpin' Jacket

David Nelson Nelson

Junket. There were many more of those junkets and the worst one of all was fantastic.

Tom never gave it a thought when he parked outside some girl's house while I was inside making out or just talking. He enjoyed listening to *WLS Radio Station* out of Chicago on his transistor radio that hung from the rear view mirror. He always asked for details of the events, which I obliged. After all, he was my pal.

PALS: Part One

"The Empty Pear Tree"

The eleventh grade in high school continued with delinquent behavior that began two years earlier. I was sad, irate, and lonely inside. I suppose that is why I focused so heavily on being accepted by both girls and boys. I did the bare minimum in class despite Veronica's encouragement during our weekly phone calls. I excelled in track and field and continued to be unbeaten in the 100 and 220-yard dashes. Kosta, Veronica, Jim, and Tom attended all home meets to watch Rex and me compete. My parents *never* saw me compete. I gave up trying to be like Rex and my brother, Richard. I knew there was no way I could make the honor roll, be on student council, and be popular like "I saw" the two of them. The days of lying under the pear tree in Rex's backyard, discussing future plans were over. Like rotted fruit that fell to the ground, such was my position in life. I had nothing but Tom, his family, and my speed. Or so I thought.

During the spring of that year two events occurred that changed my life. It was in the spring of 1966, when I answered the phone and said, "Nelson residence."

"Is Dave there?"

"This is he."

"This is your father, Richard."

"No, you have the wrong number," I said and hung up.

Seconds later it rang again and the stranger said, "Don't hang up this time. I am Richard Salzmann and I am your natural father. I would like to meet you. Could you come to Gross Papa's and Gross Mama's house for dinner?"

I was numb. I was in shock. I felt sick but curiosity had me and I agreed to meet him. I hung up the phone went into the bathroom and threw up. All those years I received Christmas presents from someone named Dick came crashing into me like a switch engine on the railroad tracks. I remembered asking as a kid, "Who is Dick?"

I was told not to ask questions and just open the present. In time I accepted it as if he were some distant relative. I mentioned earlier that secrets were kept from outsiders during the 1950s and 1960s. This was one kept among family members. Ma made certain of that.

After hanging up the phone and vomiting in the bathroom, I walked to the garage to call Veronica and tell her what I discovered. I still had an upset stomach when she answered the phone. "Hello." "You are not going to believe what just happened to me."

She screamed into the phone each of the three times she asked me to repeat the story. I could tell she was crying and then laughing. I knew my friend was happy for me. Veronica came to my house that week and took me across town to my grandparent's home. She reached across the seat and squeezed my hand. "Good luck. Call me."

I was nervous and excited the night I met Dick at Gross Papa's house. On the one hand I was really upset that I did not know this person and wondered why he had abandoned me. On the other hand I wondered if he might be here to take me away from this awful place called home. I remember little of that night other than just a few events.

He told me how he was a Lutheran minister and a former missionary in New Guinea. He showed me slides of that country and I specifically remember the blood beetle. He said the natives would eat the beetles full of blood found in dry riverbeds during the dry season. I was impressed. He said he was a writer and the Editor-in-Chief of something called the Research Institute of America. Again, I was impressed. He said he was the quarterback for Senior High School where he graduated and had pretty good speed. And then, I was really impressed.

PALS: Part One

When he took me home that night, we parked in the dark on Lincoln Avenue. I spoke of the upcoming prom dance. He gave me fifty-dollars for the event and a hug. He said we would now stay in contact. I never saw him again until 1988 when I re-married for the third time. That's correct, folks. I had two failed marriages and two children that I have not seen in years. A cycle is going on here.

My older siblings knew all about Dick and simply figured I did also. My younger siblings did not discover this secret until the funeral of my step-dad, whom I considered my real dad. That was in 1986. Ma did a great job of keeping secrets.

She was not the only one. Remember when I mentioned about Rex taking a German class from Miss Reu at Senior High School? Remember how I told you my great grandfather's name was Reu? Remember how I said my older brother's middle name was Reu? Put it all together. Rex's German teacher was the sister of Gross Mama and therefore my great aunt. I never knew this until age 62. Secrets can be tough.

It was that same spring the last time I was beaten up at home. The abuse started at about age eight and the last abuse was at age seventeen. I was grounded again, that May in 1967. I was a senior in high school. I broke the ultimate rule. I left the house to run at the Iowa State Track Meet held at the Drake University stadium in Des Moines, Iowa. Rex was a great sprinter and broad jumper on our track team. He gave me a run for the money in the 100 and 220-yard dashes. A couple weeks before State Finals, he pulled a hamstring and was unable to run on our team. That was too bad because he deserved to be there that day. We broke a school record in the 440-yard relay that was set in 1942. Our record at Senior High School has never been beaten. We won first place in that event at the State Meet. All the other kids had a grand time riding home to Dubuque. I remember sitting quietly looking out the window of my coach's car as the miles passed by. There was an awful burn in my stomach thinking of what was to come.

David Nelson Nelson

I inhaled as deeply as I could, walked into the house, and forced a smile. "Look, we won first place." I held up the medal and the belt buckle knocked it from my grip.

Dad's fist hit the center of my chest and knocked me to the floor. The stinging pain from being beaten with a belt buckle made me scream. I pushed my face into the dirty carpet and curled into a ball. I escaped mentally while he continued to flail away at me. I was crying and screaming on the outside, but inside I noticed the stink of spilled booze, dirty feet and dog feces ground into the carpet. I thought about the screaming from spectators at the track meet just a few hours earlier. I had mastered the survival of mentally escaping long before that night! While being tortured I managed to smile to myself knowing that I would go to college and get away from the abuse. I had met the goal I set at age eight to leave and never return. He never hit me again. Sometimes in life, timing is everything.

Ma sat there smoking and chugging on her Hamm's Beer watching without emotion.

"The War"

It was a cool, rainy Sunday evening as my family and I watched the Ed Sullivan Show on television. The program was interrupted by the sound of the doorbell. It was Kosta. It was a rare occasion for any of my friends to actually enter my home. I was only inside a couple friends' homes. For the most part I avoided most of the homes of others. There might have been an alcoholic parent on a rampage, an older brother pissed-off and wanting to fight, or just an unwelcome attitude from parents.

I offered Kosta a seat on the burnt orange colored davenport and was curious as to what caused him to come to my house that night. The others in the room were focused on the television and my sister turned up the volume as Kosta and I chatted about trivial things. His left elbow leaned against the arm of the davenport while his palm held his head. I could tell something was amiss.

Out of nowhere, he quietly spoke. "My brother, Ellis was killed in Vietnam."

The television was turned off immediately. All of us were in shock. We did not know what to say. We did not know how to offer comfort. I don't remember anything else about that evening. I don't remember what else was said. I don't remember Kosta leaving. I do remember feeling badly for him as I do to this day.

It was no more than a month later that Jim's brother, Mike was killed in Vietnam as well. I remember Mike playing a song on a 45rpm record where some of the lyrics were: *"If ya wanna be happy for the rest of your life, get an ugly girl to be your wife."* That was a couple weeks before he shipped out to the war.

Many kids from the North End of Dubuque went to war. Not all were killed. Eddie was a Green Beret who lost both legs. Jack was a gunner in a helicopter who came home leaving his right arm in Vietnam. There were Chris, Whitey, Rob, another kid named

David Nelson Nelson

Tom, and Geno, Frank, and Jack, and many others. Some did well in life and managed to meld back into society but some did not.

There were thirty-two bodies that were sent back to the Dubuqueland area from Vietnam. A 33rd person is still missing. I knew several of these young men from the North End. There was Daniel Chatfield, Lawrence Hilkin, Richard Sutherland, Gerald Kinny, William Juergens, Ellas Mihalakis, and Mike Clemens. Should you ever visit Dubuque, Iowa, be sure to visit the Vietnam Memorial where you will find the entire list. It's along the river near the old Camp Seventeen.

PALS: Part One

"Beyond Pomp and Circumstance"

After graduation Rex went away to Augustana College in Rock Island, Illinois. Kosta joined the navy and I lost track of both of them for several years. Jim entered the work force and he and I also lost track of one another. Tom and I remained friends and it was a tough day for me to say good-bye to him as I left Dubuque for the University of Northern Iowa in Cedar Falls. I was given a track scholarship because of the efforts of Coach Udelhoff at Jefferson Junior High School. I had met my long-time goal. Veronica also attended The University of Northern Iowa.

One of my friends from Senior High was my roommate along with another kid neither of us knew but quickly came to like. My Dubuque roommate was an Irish Catholic kid who grew up a couple blocks from my wealthy Uncle Clem near Wartburg Seminary.

During the winter he and I were given a ride back to Cedar Falls after spending a weekend in Dubuque. Gross Papa drove us. At one point I needed to use the restroom so we pulled over at a gas station. When I came out I noticed my roommate was different and quiet. Back at the dorm he said, "Do you know what your grandfather told me when you went to the john?"

"No, what?"

"He asked why I was corrupting his grandson and I should be going to a Catholic school like Loras. He said I was no good for you."

I will not print the words I used that Sunday evening in room 305 at Baker Hall. After I verbally vented, I sat down and wrote a letter to Gross Papa. I told him in no uncertain words how I felt he was a bigot and I never wanted to see him again. I told him that he disgusted me and I hated the day we ever met. That was the last communication I had with him. I never saw my Gross Papa or Gross Mama again. I never went to their funerals.

Years of being locked away in an emotional prison at home and then having freedom sprung on me were almost more than I could comprehend. All I knew was that I was a star athlete at a major university and considered myself special. Deep inside, however, the years of physical abuse, the lack of maternal nurturing, lies, abandonment, anxiety, and depression made me a wreck. I had no business being in college.

In addition to my scholarship, I was given a job as a janitor at the gymnasium. I had to work because my parents never gave me a dime for school. Each morning I had to clean the pool, scrub locker rooms, or clean the hallways before class. The key word here is *before*. I figured I was so special I didn't have to attend classes. You guessed it. At the end of the first semester I was on probation but kept my scholarship. By the end of the first year I was politely asked not to return. I blew my one chance in life. My depression mounted as I returned home.

One day I was sitting on the glider on Tom's front porch. His dad came outside, sat next to me and lit a cigarette. He cleared his throat. "Son, you have disappointed me. You have disappointed all my family. You had a gift and you blew it. I am very ashamed of you."

He stood, flicked his cigarette into the very bushes where years earlier I hid and played my trombone. He walked back into the house and locked the door. That door was never locked before. Not since the ninth grade when Jane Reid told me I disappointed her, had I felt such shame. I walked down the steps of the porch and I was alone, completely alone.

It was at that moment I promised myself I would change my life and make a difference. Somehow. Someway.

Epilogue

David Nelson Nelson

The first third of my life has been described in *PALS: Part One*. If you enjoyed it, tell your friends. If you did not, keep it our little secret. I would be remiss if I did not explain certain aspects of my book to you.

All the events I wrote about happened to me. All of them. In some of the stories, I included my pals as part of the experience. In many instances, however, my pals were not actually involved, but other people I knew were. I wrote the book in this fashion to allow for literary continuity. Some examples where my pals didn't actually do the things I related included: Tom and I stealing cigarettes from the grocery store; Rex hopping a train and jumping off the train bridge; none of my pals were with me when I stole the bowling ball; Kosta didn't harass Henry about his rabbits. They weren't those types of people. And so I shall leave it up to each of them to tell the actual truths to their families and friends. Oh, by the way, Kosta does not have diabetes nor did he win the "peeing contest". That was another kid.

I have "ized" my first twenty years of life to death. I analyzed, theorized, scrutinized, poeticized and hypothesized my life until there was no more to address. Yes, I was a victim of physical and emotional child abuse. But to that end, I can now say, "So what?" It has made me who I am today. Yes, I have suffered from clinical depression most of my life. But to that end, I can now say, "So what?"

I embrace all the pieces of my life, as they are what make me special. I like who I am and no longer do I look back and blame anyone else for my mental health issues of depression and anxiety. It is what it is. And it was what it was. I was a thug, a delinquent and someone who, in pain and anger, struck back at society. But I'm not now: I'm not a thug and am too old to be a delinquent. And I like society too much to strike back. I am so pleased I outgrew my poor behavior and bad attitude.

Or did I?

PALS: Part One

In *PALS: Part Two,* I will answer that question where this book left off. Read it to discover if I made a difference in society and to the world in general. Read it and learn what happened as a result of the solemn promise I made to myself at age eight. You will learn what happened to a poor kid from the North End of Dubuque, Iowa. Just as the original Pals helped me for the first twenty years of life, you'll meet another Pal, who in adult life was just as important as Veronica, Rex, Jim, Kosta and Tom were to me in young adulthood.

"One should... be able to see that things are hopeless and yet be determined to make them otherwise." F. Scott Fitzgerald from, "The Crack-up"

<u>Appendix</u>

PALS: Part One

The Many Faces of David Nelson Nelson

Photo by Dr. Ellen Rudolph

David Nelson Nelson

North End of Dubuque Then and Now

Sewer-Where Tom and I shot unsuspecting public with our bean shooters. He was the original **PAL**.

Tom Schweikert's House- 2126 Kniest Street. We threw watermelons from the roof at passerbys, constructed a bomb, I played a trombone hidden in the bushes and I found sanctuary as my second home.

Linwood Cemetery-The place where I once hid in a fresh-dug grave, playing hide-and-seek at night.

Lock and Dam-In the spring I once walked from the Iowa side to the Wisconsin side of the thawing Mississippi River.

PALS: Part One

North End of Dubuque Then and Now

Railroad Bridge-At age fourteen I jumped off this train bridge into the Mississippi River. The bridge connects Dubuque Iowa and East Dubuque, Illinois.

Sacred Heart Catholic Church-The bells from this church could be heard everyday at noon and six throughout the North End.

Shot Tower-Dubuque Civil War Shot Tower, located near the former Johnny Petrakis Baseball Complex. It was here that I was a member of the Knot-Hole Club and shagged balls beyond the fence.

617 Lincoln Avenue-Here is a sketch of my boyhood home at 617 Lincoln Avenue in Dubuque Iowa. The lot size of our house was 26 feet wide and 138 feet long. It was built in 1890.

David Nelson Nelson

North End of Dubuque Then and Now

Audubon Elementary School-1854-1973. I attended this school from kindergarten through sixth grade. I returned in 2012 to entertain and educate third graders in my old school about the cowboy way of life.

Jefferson Junior High School-I attended school grades seven throug nine and I met the remaining **PALS** in seventh grade.

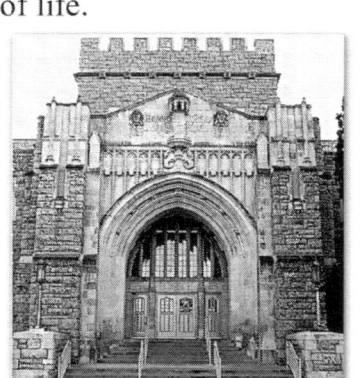

Dubuque Senior High School-Founded in 1858. I attended grades ten through twelve.

Wartburg Theological Seminary-My grandfather, Samuel Salzmann, taught Homiletics at the Seminary for numerous decades.
My great grandfather, Johann Michael Reu, taught every course offered during his tenure from 1899-1943. The library is named the Reu Memorial Library in his honor.

256

David Nelson Nelson's Other Books

The Shade Tree Choir

Krame suffers the physical and emotional abuse from his alcoholic parents and mentally ill mother for nearly ten years. As a child, he promises himself he will leave the deprived area and never return. As an eight year old, Krame finds solace with three of his cohorts. He is known by the gang as the "Thinker" because he plans every escapade to the finest detail so they will never get caught. Little do the other three know, Krame does not want to be caught and suffer another beating at home. Things go on like this until tragedy strikes.

The grim truth of Krame's childhood stays hidden for forty years until he opens up to one of his old friends when he returns home to bury his father. In the process of remembering and opening up about his past, Krame discovers his dad was not who he thought he was.

Campfire Collection of Cowpoke Poetry

Author, David Nelson is the Cowboy Poet Laureate of Tennessee. He has performed across America and now brings his performing art into written form. You will laugh, cry, and think as he writes on array of topics common to all people. He also has a storytelling section about his wife, whom he nicknames "Trixie". Poems in the book can be read around a campfire or a dinner table. The content is appropriate for all ages (except) the story called the Psychiatrist. David Nelson is known as the 'Biggest Liar in East Tennessee' so read along and try to figure what is fact and what is fiction. Either way he hopes you 'laugh 'till you leak'.

Coming Soon

Be sure to watch for the sequel, "PALS: Part Two"

Made in the USA
San Bernardino, CA
25 June 2014